**BARCODE ON
NEXT PAGE**

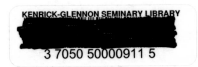
So, Where'd You Go to High School?

Volume 1:

Affton to Yeshiva: 200 Years of St. Louis Area High Schools

By Ray Bosenbecker

2005-0076

So, Where'd You Go to High School?
Volume 1:
Affton to Yeshiva:
200 Years of St. Louis Area High Schools
By Ray Bosenbecker

Cover Design: Michael Kilfoy
Book Design & Layout: Susan K. Nelson

First Edition
Copyright © 2004 by Ray Bosenbecker

ISBN: 1-891442-30-9
Library of Congress Control Number: 2004111045

IRGINIA PUBLISHING CO.

Virginia Publishing Co.
P.O. Box 4538
St. Louis, MO 63108
314-367-6612

www.STL-BOOKS.com

This book is dedicated to:

Donna Jean Carriere Bosenbecker,
Southwest High School

Jennifer Rae Bosenbecker Bruner,
Parkway North High School

Mary McCready Bosenbecker Burkemper,
Parkway North High School

Raymond William Bosenbecker III,
Parkway West High School

Anne Carriere Bosenbecker,
Parkway West High School

Margaret Elizabeth Raible Bosenbecker,
Tuley High School, Chicago

Raymond William Bosenbecker, Sr.,
Lane Technical High School, Chicago

All the people who constructed, attended, taught,
managed, or helped St. Louis-area high schools

Acknowledgments

Donna Bosenbecker

Sharon Huffman
St. Louis Public Schools Archivist

Audrey Newcomer
Director of Archives, Archdiocese of St. Louis

Suzanne Muther
Reviewer

Fran Levy
Editor

Jeff Fister
Publisher

Mark Bremer
Reviewer

Contents

INTRODUCTION

1

CHAPTER 1

Early Education in St. Louis: 1774

5

CHAPTER 2

Impact of the Civil War on Education: 1861 – 1900

11

CHAPTER 3

*1904 World's Fair and Its Impact on
High Schools: 1900 – 1920*

15

CHAPTER 4

St. Louis High School Architects

21

CHAPTER 5

St. Louis Neighborhoods and Their High Schools

29

CHAPTER 6

Vocational High Schools: 1920 – 2004

35

CHAPTER 7
St. Louis-Area County High Schools
37

CHAPTER 8
*Impact of Civil Rights and Desegregation on
High Schools: 1955 – 2004*
57

CHAPTER 9
Specialized Schools: 1800 – 2004
65

CHAPTER 10
High Schools in the New Millennium
71

CHAPTER 11
Future High Schools
73

APPENDIX
COMPENDIUM OF ST. LOUIS-AREA HIGH SCHOOLS
Public High Schools 75
Parochial High Schools 123
Independent High Schools 153

MAPS
160

BIBLIOGRAPHY
172

INDEX
174

Introduction

In 1965, I graduated from college and arrived in St. Louis for an engineering position at McDonnell Aircraft Company. After becoming acquainted with friends born in St. Louis, I became fascinated with the importance they placed on where someone went to high school. Through the years, I learned bits and pieces of St. Louis high school history from my wife, four children, friends and business associates.

St. Louis is a city rich in history, and many books have been written about it. Some provide limited information on the schools and educational institutions developed through the 240 years of St. Louis's recorded history. However, I have never found a book that was written solely about high schools. The intent of this book is to provide a short history of high school development in St. Louis, followed by a brief description of the more than 150 past and present high schools and those under construction in St. Louis City and St. Louis County. The high schools will be listed in alphabetical order in one of the three following categories: public, parochial or independent. If a school was accidentally omitted or some of the details are incorrect, I apologize.

M y purpose in writing this book is to leave a legacy to the people who live in St. Louis. It is my hope that this book will renew interest in all our high schools by sharing their stories that describe how obstacles were overcome and how much high schools have developed through the years. Prior to the establishment of public high schools, secondary schools were a means to educate children only from very wealthy families; today they are available for everyone. I hope the knowledge gained from reading this book will build bridges of communication and trust across generations and among family, friends, students and teachers. And finally, I hope it will be a catalyst for accomplishing even greater breakthroughs in the field of secondary education in the future.

Ray was born and raised in Chicago and graduated from Lane Technical High School in 1961. After graduating from Purdue University with a BSEE in 1965, he moved to St. Louis, began his engineering career at McDonnell Aircraft Company and met his future wife and inspiration for this book. While at McDonnell, he attended evening classes at University of Missouri at Rolla Extension and received an MSEM in 1970. Ray and Donna (maiden name Carriere) have four children:  *Jennifer Rae, Mary McCready, Ray III(deceased) and Anne Carriere. Since coming to St. Louis, Ray has been involved in youth and community activities through Jaycees, CC Days, Creve Coeur Squires, Youth Soccer, Ulster Project, and Habitat for Humanity. Ray is an engineer at Boeing and recently was selected as a Boeing Technical Fellow. This is his first book.*

Where did you go to school?

Nowhere in the world does the answer to this simple question mean as much as it does in St. Louis. The answer to this simple question often describes where you lived, your friends, neighborhood, parent's occupation, family income, your house, church, activities, ethnic background, age, college you would attend, type of person you would marry, and your future. And this is just the beginning.

High school has always been much more than the school that follows grammar school. For many in the late 19th, 20th and even the 21st centuries, it was the culmination of a lifetime goal. Chances are that for you and others in the later part of the 20th century it was in high school that you moved beyond your neighborhood boundaries. It was there that you had a chance to participate in sports, the arts, science or shop, receive recognition for your accomplishments, or lead others. It was there that you met people different from you, began to think for yourself, had tough decisions to make, became an adult, had your first date, learned to drive a car, began your first job, decided on a career, went to war, and perhaps met your future wife or husband, or obtained your final formal education. So many significant and memorable things are wrapped up in the few years of high school, it's no wonder that your school, your memories, and the people you met there have such a strong influence on you for the rest of your life.

Chapter 1

Early Education in St. Louis: 1774

On February 15, 1764, when he was just 14 years old, René Auguste Chouteau founded St. Louis. Earlier, young Chouteau had visited the site of the future city with his mentor, Pierre de Laclède. Under directions from Laclède, he led a working party from Maxent, Laclède, and Company of New Orleans to build a city on the Mississippi for the trading company. St. Louis's earliest inhabitants were Indians and French trappers.

Chouteau was born in New Orleans on September 17, 1750, and how much formal education he had when he founded St. Louis is unknown; but, as he lived in the 18th century, it's unlikely that he had any formal schooling. Most of his education, including his ability to read and write, probably was obtained from on-the-job training, listening to his mother and father and to Laclède, and observing others. The skills needed to found a city were manifest, and his ability to read and write set him apart from others in the group. He had to be a leader, linguist, navigator, engineer, doctor, carpenter and much more.

It's ironic that the first person described in a book about high schools never went to one and was barely old enough to attend one. Yet, young Chouteau accomplished more in a few years than most highly educated people accomplish in a lifetime. After contemplating Chouteau's accomplishments, it makes one wonder about the tremendous capability and potential each of us has even before entering high school, and how much more we should be able to do after we complete high school.

Chouteau and his half-brother, Jean Pierre, built an extensive business and a virtual monopoly of trade with the Osage Indians along the Missouri River and its tributaries. On September 21, 1786, Chouteau married Marie Therèse Cerre, who was born at Kaskaskia, Illinois, on November 26, 1769. After Pierre Laclède died in 1778, the Laclède/Maxent house fell into disrepair. In 1789, Chouteau purchased the house and its surrounding land. He repaired, enlarged, remodeled and furnished the home in such a grand style that it soon became the showplace of the area. He and Marie Therèse lived in the house and entertained in elegant style until his death on February 24, 1829. His wife continued to live in the house for several more years; she died on August 14, 1842. In 1841 the house, located at Rue d'Eglise and the public market, was torn down to make room for commercial buildings.

The first St. Louis elementary school opened in 1774, when Jean Baptiste Truteau founded a school for the sons of the wealthy who were able to pay for education. This was followed by a succession of other private elementary schools.

The early secondary schools of Missouri were broadly classified as chartered and uncharted academies and high schools; the academies included the boys' Academy, Female

Seminary, coeducational Academy and some military schools. These institutions were controlled by Boards of Trustees. Some were chartered by the state and funded by tuition fees, donations, and – in some cases – by the receipt of public lands in consideration for educating poor children in the district. Seminaries generally were organized as boarding schools.

In 1818, three years before Missouri became a state, the first Catholic high school was founded. It began as St. Louis Academy, but in 1924 was incorporated as "St. Louis University High School." Other early examples of early secondary schools were: Visitation Academy; St. Joseph Academy; Ursuline Academy; Bridgeton Academy (chartered in 1864); St. Charles Military Academy in St. Charles; Kirkwood Military Academy; and Kirkwood Seminary for girls.

The Louisiana Purchase in 1803 incorporated the City of St. Louis into the United States of America. Thomas Jefferson's famous land deal cost $15,000,000 for an area of 828,000 square miles that extended from New Orleans to Canada – including all or most of what would become Louisiana, Arkansas, Oklahoma, Missouri, Kansas, Colorado, Iowa, Nebraska, Wyoming, Minnesota, North and South Dakota and Montana. As a result of the purchase, St. Louis became the capital of what was known as the "Upper Louisiana Territory."

March 10, 1804, was a unique day in St. Louis history: St. Louis was the site of a three-flag treaty signing involving France, Spain and the United States. First, Spain signed over the Upper Louisiana Territory to France, and then France deeded it immediately to the United States.

In 1812, Missouri was established as a territory, and the U. S. Congress specified that unclaimed land be set aside for the support of schools. Missouri became a state on August 10, 1821. A condition for statehood known as the "Missouri Compromise" required that Missouri be admitted as a slave state, and that every future state north of Missouri's southern border be admitted as a free state. In time, Missouri became surrounded by free states, except for those at its southern borders.

The first St. Louis public school, an elementary school located at Fourth and Spruce Streets, opened in 1838. It was originally called "Schoolhouse No. 1," but in 1851 the name was changed to "Laclède Primary" in honor of Pierre Laclède (1724-1778), co-founder of St. Louis. The school closed in 1860.

In 1847, the Missouri Legislature passed a law that prohibited blacks from learning to read, write or assemble in public.

The 1850s were exciting years for St. Louis and its public education system. St. Louis was a center for fur trading, cattle and tobacco and became the eighth largest city in the country. Its population more than doubled from 1850 to 1860. In those 10 years, the number of public school students increased from 2,100 to 12,166, and St. Louis's first public high school opened in 1853. Because of pressing needs and a limited budget, an existing elementary school house, known as "Benton School" (also known as "Schoolhouse Number 3"), was selected to house the first public high school in the city of St. Louis. It was located on Sixth Street between Locust and St. Charles Streets.

Early St. Louis schools were staffed with teachers educated in the more developed eastern states or in Europe. Many teachers, after working for a year or two in St. Louis, quit and returned to their homes in the east to teach because they missed their families, friends and activities back home. Wealthy St. Louis families usually hired tutors to educate their children privately at home. Some attended the few private schools in St. Louis, or more than likely went to high schools in the eastern part of the country or in Europe.

One very famous product of the St. Louis educational system was Susan Elizabeth Blow, who was born in St. Louis in 1843. Susan was the daughter of one of St Louis's most prominent business and political families and was given the finest private education available. When her family decided that the education was inadequate, her father hired a teacher from Philadelphia and started a school for Susan and some of her friends. When she became 16, Susan traveled to New York for more training, and in the next few years she also studied in Brazil. In 1871, Susan returned to St. Louis, and for a short time taught as a substitute teacher in the public schools. She left again in 1872 to study teaching techniques in the east, and in 1873 she returned to St. Louis. Under the encouragement of Superintendent Harris, Susan Blow opened America's first public kindergarten at Des Peres School in Carondelet. Susan was influenced by the methods described by German educator and founder of the Kindergarten system, Friedrich Froebel (1782-1852).

The school board recognized the need to develop a means to train and develop teachers for St. Louis schools and established the Normal School in 1857. The teacher-training program became so effective that, within the next two decades, St. Louis had a surplus of teachers.

High schools reflect the value a community places on education, and I believe you will see from the following narrative the high value that St. Louis and its surrounding areas have placed on secondary education. It has taken more than 150 years and the talent, vision and dedication of many people to develop the institution, oftentimes taken for granted, called the "high school." The early high schools listed below will be described later in the book.

St. Louis University High School – 1818

St. Joseph Academy – 1840

St. Phelomena Technical School – 1845

Ursuline Academy – 1848

Christian Brothers College High School – 1850

Wyman Hall School – 1851

First public high school west of the Mississippi: Benton School – 1853

[Central] High School – 1856

Visitation Academy – 1833

Mary Institute – 1858

Academy of the Sacred Heart (City House) convent and orphanage - 1827

2 chapter

Impact of the Civil War on Education: 1861 - 1900

The beginning of the Civil War on April 12, 1861, had a significant impact on education in St. Louis. Prior to the war, citizens in Missouri, and St. Louis, in particular, were divided on the issue of slavery. The war not only polarized the City with northern sympathizers and southern sympathizers but it diverted funds earmarked for education. It created social and political division in the City, reduced the number of enrolled students (who had to assume responsibilities of relatives who went off to war), and reduced the number of available teachers. Some of the male teachers and administrators went off to fight in the war while others involved themselves in wartime businesses. Many of the female teachers worked at home and or in business activities previously held by brothers and fathers who joined the army.

After 1865, the war continued to have a significant impact on education in St. Louis, with an increase in the black population in St. Louis and a federal mandate to provide facilities to educate blacks. Between 1860 and 1880, St. Louis's black population increased from 3,927 to 22,256, primarily because of St. Louis's favorable location. The City was just up the Mississippi River from many of the slave states, and St. Louis had a reputation for providing more favorable treatment to slaves and freed slaves than they received in the South. Prior to 1865, very few blacks attended elementary schools in St. Louis, and even fewer attended high schools.

The Missouri Compromise was passed in 1820 and changed Missouri's laws regarding slaves.

In 1865, the restructured Missouri State constitution legally required education for blacks. By 1866, the St. Louis City census showed a population of 204,000, with 15,291 students enrolled in public schools.

After the Civil War, public school average daily enrollment increased from 13,926 (1864-1865) to 21,186 (1868-1869), and schools became overcrowded. As a result, beginning in 1868, the Polytechnic Building at Seventh and Chestnut shared its facilities with Central High School students and became known as a branch high school. In the following decade, several elementary schools also became branch high schools: Douglas School, at 11th and Howard Avenue (1872); Clinton School, at 1224 Grattan (1877); Peabody School, at 1606 South 18th Street (1872); and Webster School, at 12th and Jefferson (1872). The diplomas that the students received were issued by Central High School.

In 1876, the City of St. Louis separated from the County, making it necessary to establish a new school district outside the limits of the City of St. Louis.

By 1888, the City population had grown to 449,160, with 44,000 students enrolled in public schools; 1,177 of them were performing high school work. At the time, there were 36 high school teachers.

By 1890, the population of St. Louis had grown to 575,238, and St. Louis was transforming from a rural community to one of the largest cities in the Middle West.

Because of increasing demands from the black community for better education for their children, in 1875 the St. Louis Board of Education agreed to open the first African-American high school west of the Mississippi River. Initially, the black high school classes were held in a few vacant rooms in the "colored" elementary school. In 1875, Charles Sumner High School became the first black high school in the City of St. Louis when it opened in the old Washington elementary school at 11th Street and Spruce. The school remained open until 1897, when a new Charles Sumner High School was opened at 15th Street and Walnut. In the early 1900s, community leaders petitioned the Board of Education to relocate the school to a location away from the downtown poolrooms and taverns so that the students would not be unfavorably influenced by their surroundings. The new Sumner High School opened in 1910 and became the cornerstone of the historic Ville neighborhood and an anchor of the community. Sumner High School is still serving the community today.

In 1897, William B. Ittner took the job as Commissioner of School Buildings for St. Louis Public Schools and began designing some of the most beautiful schools in the United States. Ittner and his architectural firm designed 500 schools in St. Louis and around the United States, and by the 1910s Ittner's schools brought national attention for St. Louis's new schools. Even after he resigned as Commissioner of School Buildings on March 9, 1910, he continued to design St. Louis Public School buildings until 1915.

The following high schools opened between the end of the Civil War and the turn of the century.

St. Elizabeth Academy – 1882
Douglas High School –1882
Central High School (3rd location) – 1893
City House – 1893
Sumner High School - 1875

Chapter 3

1904 World's Fair and Its Impact on High Schools: 1900 - 1920

Among the positive forces responsible for renewing emphasis on St. Louis public high schools were the 1904 St. Louis World's Fair (also known as the "Louisiana Purchase Exposition") and visionary architect William B. Ittner.

The St. Louis Board of Education was eager to show the world what St. Louis had done in the area of education. The "Palace of Education," a temporary building constructed for the Fair at a cost of $365,421, was massive. At 750 feet by 525 feet, the building was longer than two football fields end-to-end and had nine acres of interior space. Inside the Palace were numerous exhibits and live displays of actual classes in session. The exhibits for technical schools from Germany, Austria, Great Britain, and Ireland were in open areas so that the visitors could actually watch the students being taught. Each day, a different St. Louis-area school was selected to bring an entire class to "The Fair," and teachers taught their class in front of a live audience. The St. Louis Public School system demonstrated kindergarten classes as well as classes that gave demonstrations in carpentry, sewing, cooking and music. Students from the Missouri School for the Deaf were taught tailoring and broom making, while students from the School for the Blind were taught piano tuning and other business trades.

The Board invited the National Education Association to St. Louis for its 1904 annual meeting and agreed to open all schoolhouses for inspection by Fair visitors. In addition, the Board provided $20,000 for an educational exhibit at the Fair. The St. Louis School Board exhibit was awarded 27 prizes by the Fair judges for its excellent features.

After the Fair, artifacts from the exhibits of participating countries were purchased by the Board and became part of an Educational Museum, which evolved into the first audio-visual department in the United States.

The World Fair's period was a time for growth and interest in education. The marvelous exhibits and technology demonstrations highlighted what education could do and illustrated the need for higher education. During this period, a number of high schools opened for the first time or moved to new locations.

"Meet Me in St. Louis," the nostalgic story about the grandeur of St. Louis at the turn of the century, is the most endearing and memorable movie ever produced about St. Louis. For most of us it evokes a feeling of pride and longing; yet, in spite of its success, it missed one of the most important aspects of St. Louis life. Although Judy Garland was magnificent as Esther Smith, the high school-age young lady who falls in love with Tom Drake, the boy next door, the movie ironically failed to answer the one question asked by St. Louis natives: "Where did you go to high school?"

The movie takes place in 1903-1904 and is based on the

book written in the 1940s by Sally Smith Benson, a native of St. Louis. Sally was only five years old in 1904, and later she and her family moved to New York City -- before Sally went to high school.

However, Esther's home at 5135 Kensington Avenue in the Cabanne neighborhood provides the clue. She lived in St. Louis City a few blocks northwest of the Kingshighway and Delmar Boulevard intersection, near the northeast corner of Forest Park, which was the home of the 1904 World's Fair.

Esther's address, religion, neighborhood and ethnicity, as well as her father's occupation and financial and social status would have had a significant impact on which high school she and her sister attended. Considering all those factors, her high school would have been Visitation Academy, the private Catholic girls' school one mile away; Mary Institute, the private girls' school four blocks away; or Central High School, the coeducational public high school three-and-a-half miles away.

The high school Esther would have attended is up to you and your imagination! Or, you can read the book to find out "where Esther Smith went to high school!"

Author's Note: In 1962, Visitation Academy, at Cabanne at Belt (1898-1962), relocated to 3020 North Ballas Road in St. Louis County. Visitation Park now stands in place of the former school, which was razed in 1962. In 1928, Mary Institute, at 455 Lake Avenue (1899-1928), relocated to 101 North Warson Road in St. Louis County. The facility at 455 Lake Avenue became New City School in 1972. In 1993, Mary Institute and St. Louis Country Day School entered into a full-scale alliance to form Mary Institute County Day School (MICDS). Central High School, at 1020 North Grand (1893-1927), was destroyed by a tornado on September 29, 1927. The students relocated to Yeatman High School, at 3616 North Garrison Avenue. Yeatman High School was renamed "Central High

School" and later Central Visual and Performing Arts School, a magnet high school. Today, Soldan International High School Studies Program, a magnet school at 918 North Union Boulevard, is the nearest high school; New City School teaches students only up to sixth grade.

Smith Academy and Manual Training School, built in 1905, was a nearby, private boys' school sponsored by Washington University for elite clientele. It was located at 5351 Enright Avenue in the Cabanne area, closed in 1917, and sold to the St. Louis Board of Education. Many schools used the building: Christian Brothers College High School after the fire (1916); Ben Blewett Junior High School (1918-1931); Ben Blewett High School (1931-1948); Harris Teachers College (1948-1963); and Enright Middle School (1963). (In 1975 it became Enright Ninth Grade Center as a supplement to Soldan High School.) The building still exists but has been sold by the St. Louis School District.

The following high school buildings opened between 1900 and 1920.

McKinley High School – 1904

Yeatman High School – 1904

Smith Academy and Manual Training School – 1905

Soldan High School – 1909

Sumner High School (3rd location) – 1875

Chaminade College Preparatory School – 1910

Principia High School – 1910

Rosati-Kain High School – 1912

Barat Hall For Boys – 1913

Cleveland High School – 1915

Poro College – 1917

St. Louis Country Day School -1917

4 Chapter

St. Louis High School Architects

Much of the success of St. Louis high schools is due to the contributions made by the architects who designed the schools. They created buildings that influenced the design of high schools all over the United States. Of all these architects, the best known was William Butts Ittner. This chapter provides a brief description of the St. Louis high school architects and the buildings they designed.

William Butts Ittner

William Butts Ittner was born in St. Louis in 1864, the first child of Anthony and Mary Butts Ittner. William's father left school at the age of 9 and worked in a lead factory, then as a bricklayer, and then finally established Ittner Brothers Brick Company with his brother Conrad in 1859. In 1867, Anthony was elected to the City Council and, in 1877, to Congress. Throughout his career, he worked to establish trade schools for American young men.

Anthony's son William attended the old Manual Training School, a division of Washington University, and then entered

Cornell University. After graduation in 1887, he traveled in Europe and then returned to St. Louis, married Lottie Crand Allen, and began working for Eames and Young. Between 1889 and 1891, he practiced alone, and then entered brief partnerships, first with William Foster and then with Link and Rosenheim. Ittner was President of the St. Louis Chapter of the American Institute of Architects from 1893-1895.

On June 27, 1897, he was elected to the new office of Commissioner of School Building for the City of St. Louis. At the time he became Commissioner, one of his responsibilities was designing the schools for St. Louis. He served in that position until he resigned in 1910, but he continued as a "consulting architect" to the Board until October 1914. This remarkable relationship between St. Louis Schools and Ittner occurred at a time when some of the most revolutionary designs were created and beautiful schools built.

Perhaps because he was born and raised in St. Louis and was a product of the unimaginative, ugly, dank schools, he used his talent and position to change the traditional way that schools were designed and built. His designs changed schools from traditionally vertical buildings to more expansive, horizontal structures that were open and that centered on central gymnasiums or auditoriums. The schools were designed to use natural sunlight as part of the architectural style and to be more functional. The new schools were safer in the event of a fire and more beautiful to the casual observer. On the outside, ornamental accouterments, such as towers, turrets, domes, bay windows, statues, and reliefs, as well as location and beautifully landscaped grounds, added to the beauty of Ittner's high schools. William B. Ittner left a rich legacy in the schools he designed for St. Louis. When he died in January 1936, he had designed the following high schools and grammar schools in the St. Louis area.

McKinley High School
opened in 1904 and located at 3156 Russell Avenue

Yeatman High School
(renamed Central High School in 1928)
opened in 1904 and located at 3616 North Garrison Avenue

Soldan High School
opened in 1909 and located at 918 North Union Boulevard

Sumner High School
opened in 1910 and located at 4248 Cottage Avenue

Cleveland High School
opened in 1915 and located at 4352 Louisiana Avenue

Maplewood High School
opened in 1909 and located at 7539 Manchester Road

Pattonville High School
opened in 1935 and located at Banks and
St. Charles Rock Road

The 43 Ittner-designed elementary schools are:

Ashland
Baden, Blow, Bryan Hill
Carr, Clark, Clay, Cote Brilliant
Delany
Eliot, Emerson
Fanning, Farragut, Field, Franklin
Gardenville, Glasgow (later Dunbar)
Hempstead, Henry, Horace Mann, Humboldt
Jackson
Laclede, Lafayette, Lyon
Madison, Mark Twain, Marshall, Meramec
Monroe, Mullanphy

Normal (Harris Teachers College and
then Audio-Visual Service)
Oak Hill
Rock Spring
Shaw, Shepard, Sherman, Sigel, Simmons
Taussig Open Air
Walnut Park, Webster, Wyman

Except for Taussig Open Air School, all of the other buildings still exist.

In addition, he designed about 500 other schools across the country. Ittner created a style of form and function that influenced the design of many future St. Louis high schools.

Rockwell M. Milligan

Rockwell M. Milligan (1868-1929) continued the tradition by designing his own unique and beautiful high schools in St. Louis. Milligan was a Canadian architect who studied at Garfield University in Kansas. He trained under Isaac Taylor and was Chief Draftsman for William B. Ittner when the latter was Commissioner of School Building for the City of St. Louis from 1914 -1929. Milligan died September 30, 1929. Some of the high schools he designed are:

Roosevelt High School
opened in 1925 and located at 3240 Hartford

Beaumont High School
opened in 1926 and located at 3836 Natural Bridge

Vashon High School
opened in 1927 and located at 3026 Laclede Avenue

Barnett, Haynes and Barnett

Barnett, Haynes and Barnett designed Visitation Academy,

built in 1892 and located at the southeast corner of Cabanne and Belt Avenues. Later, George Barnett designed one of the buildings at the 1904 St. Louis World's Fair and was the chief architect for the St. Louis Cathedral Basilica on Lindell Boulevard.

Bonsack and Pierce, Incorporated

Bonsack and Pierce, Incorporated, designed Hancock Place Senior High School, which opened in 1934 at 229 West Ripa Avenue.

Marcel Boulicult

Marcel Boulicult designed Bayless High School, which opened in 1935 on Weber Road.

Parsons Brickerhoff

Parsons Brickerhoff designed Pattonville High School Library at 2497 Creve Coeur Mill Road. The firm is located at 1831 Chestnut Street in St. Louis City; the phone number is 314-421-1476.

Furlong and Brown

Furlong and Brown designed Central High School, which opened in 1893 and is located at 1020 North Grand Avenue at Finney. *Note:* it has been reported that architect Isaac Taylor was selected to finalize the design.

Gale A. Hill and Associates, Inc.

Gale A. Hill and Associates, Inc. designed Pattonville High School Auditorium, located at 2497 Creve Coeur Mill Road. The firm is located at 1560 Woodlake Drive in Creve Coeur; the phone number is 314-421-1476.

Hellmuth and Hellmuth

Hellmuth and Hellmuth designed City House, which

opened in 1893 on Taylor Avenue.

HOK

Hellmuth Obata Kassabaum is located at 1 Metropolitan Square in St. Louis City; the phone number is 314-421-2000. They designed:

St. Louis Priory School - 1973

Parkway Junior and Senior High School
opened in 1958 and located at 471 Woods Mill Road

Mitchell Hudgeback

Mitchell Hudgeback is located at 175 South Mason Road in Town and Country. The firm designed:

Chesterfield Day School, St. Albans – 1998
Whitfield School – 1952

Charles Huning

Architect Charles Huning designed Northwest High School, which opened in 1964.

Murphy and Mackey

Murphy and Mackey designed Bishop DuBourg High School, which opened in 1954.

William B. Ittner, Incorporated

William B. Ittner, Incorporated, is located at 611 North 10th Street in St. Louis City; the phone number is 314-421-3542. The firm designed:

Clayton High School
opened in 1952 at 1 Mark Twain Circle

Ritenour Senior High School
opened in 1950 at 9100 St. Charles Rock Road

Kennedy Associates, Inc.

Kennedy Associates, Inc., designed Vashon High School, which opened in 2003. The firm is located at 1 Metropolitan Square in St. Louis City; the phone number is 314-241-8188.

Victor K. Klutho

Victor Klutho designed:

Chaminade College Preparatory School, opened in 1910

LaBeaume and Klein

LaBeaume and Klein designed:

John Burroughs School, opened in 1923

F. Ray Leimkuehler

F. Ray Leimkuehler designed O'Fallon Technical High School, which opened in 1956 at 5101 Northrup.

Mackey Mitchell Associates

Mackey Mitchell Associates designed the newest Christian Brothers College High School, which opened in 2003 at 1850 De LaSalle Drive. The firm is located at 800 St. Louis Union Station, Suite 200, in St. Louis City; the phone number is 314-421-1815.

Mauran, Russell and Garden

Mauran, Russell and Garden designed Smith Academy and Manual Training School (later renamed Blewett High School), which opened in 1905.

William Rumbold

William Rumbold designed the St. Louis High School (later renamed Central High School), which opened in 1856 at the northwest corner of 15th and Olive Streets.

George W. Sanger

George W. Sanger was Commissioner of School Building for the City of St. Louis from October 1, 1929 to August 31, 1930. Between 1934 and 1939 he designed:

Southwest High School
opened in 1937 at 3125 South Kingshighway

Hadley Technical High School
opened in 1931 at 3405 Bell

Stander and Sons

Stander and Sons designed DeSmet Jesuit High School, which opened in 1967 and is located at 233 North New Ballas Road.

Jack Tyrer

Jack Tyrer designed Gateway Academy in Chesterfield, which opened in 1992.

Kenneth Wischmeyer

Ken Wischmeyer designed:

Northview School – 1964
Lutheran High School North – 1965

Kenneth E. Wischmeyer and Partners

Kenneth E. Wischmeyer and Partners designed South County Technical High School, which opened in 1967.

5 Chapter

St. Louis Neighborhoods and Their High Schools

On April 6, 1917, the United States entered the War in Europe, and there was an immediate impact on high schools across the country.

The war effort diverted funds earmarked for education and reduced the number of teachers and enrolled students. Many joined the military service or assumed some of the responsibilities of relatives who went off to war; this reduced the number of available teachers. Some of the male teachers and administrators joined the military service or worked in wartime businesses. Some of the female teachers ran business activities previously run by husbands, brothers and fathers who went off to war, and some joined the military service.

If St. Louis were compared to a building, its neighborhoods would be the bricks. St. Louis could never have grown and become one of the major cities in America without its neighborhoods. For more than a century, as the number of diverse, closely knit neighborhoods grew in population, so did St. Louis. Some neighborhoods, such as Lafayette Park and The Hill, had well-defined physical boundaries, while the boundaries for other neighborhoods, such as Dogtown, Kerry Patch or Old North St. Louis, were more ambiguous. Nonetheless, everyone came from a neighborhood and was identified by it.

The neighborhood identified not only where you lived, but much about who you were. It identified the kind of house you lived in, where your ancestors came from, your religious background, your dress code, your likely employer, where you shopped, played and went to school, whom you associated with, where you would live when you grew up, and whom you would marry. In many cases, virtually everything about you could be determined by knowing the neighborhood where you lived.

As the importance of higher education increased, more high schools were built, and enrollment of high school students reached all-time highs. Soon, the name of the high school replaced the name of the neighborhood in identifying who you were. *The high school and its geographic boundaries, instead of the neighborhood and its boundaries, became the new criterion for identifying who you were.*

The transition from neighborhood to high school labeling was gradual. No precise time or event has ever been identified as to when the high schools replaced the neighborhood in identifying a person. However, at almost the same time that neighborhood high schools were being built, the streetcar and automobile entered the scene and provided families with new levels of mobility. The family breadwinner(s) no longer were constrained by how far they had to walk to work, and the family no longer had to restrict its shopping to its own neighborhood. In time, the new anchor for the community and its geographic boundaries became the high school and its boundaries. A new high school in a neighborhood added prestige not only to its neighborhood but to the other adjoining neighborhoods embraced by its boundaries: the high school created a new geographic definition for the boundaries of the neighborhood where you were born. High schools such as Cleveland, Roosevelt, Vashon, Southwest and Soldan replaced the old boundaries previously identified by ethnic neighborhoods, such as Marquette-Cherokee, Midtown, Southwest, or Cabanne.

Just as visionary architect William B. Ittner created world-renowned St. Louis public high schools in the early 20th century, Rockwell M. Milligan (1868-1929) continued the tradition by designing his own unique and beautiful high schools in St. Louis. Some of the high schools designed by Milligan were Roosevelt High School, Beaumont High School and Vashon High School.

Early St. Louis Neighborhoods

Arlington, Baden-Riverview, Benton Park, Bissell, College Hill, Cabanne, Central West End, Central Business District, Carondelet, Clifton, Compton Heights, Fairgrounds, Grand Prairie, Hyde Park, Kingsbury, Lafayette Square, Marquette-Cherokee, Midtown, Morganford, Oak Hill, Oakland, Old North St. Louis, Southwest, The Hill, Soulard, Tower Grove, The Ville, Walnut Park, and Yeatman.

The following is a list of the high schools that were opened in the 1920s through the 1980s.

Public High Schools in St. Louis City

Roosevelt High School – 1925
Beaumont High School - 1926

Vashon High School - 1927
Blewett High School - 1933
Southwest High School – 1937
Soldan-Blewett - 1948
James B. Eads High School – 1976

The St. Louis City School District serves the City of St. Louis. The district office is located at 801 N. 11th Street in St. Louis City. The phone number is 314-231-3720 and the Website is http://www.slps.org.

During the 1930s, the decade prior to World War II, St. Louis public school average daily enrollment increased, peaking at 106,310 (1934-1935) and causing overcrowding. Since the war effort and rationing in the early 1940s prevented new construction, public elementary schools shared their facilities with high school students and became known as branch high schools. Some of the elementary schools used as branch high schools were Blow School, at 516 Loughborough Avenue (1943); Cote Brilliante School, at 2616 Cora Avenue (1943); and Wade School, at 2030 South Vandeventer (1943). The diplomas that the students received were issued by the sponsoring high school.

Other Private and Parochial High Schools in St. Louis City

New City School – 1969
Crossroads High School – 1985
Lutheran High School – 1946
Tower Grove Christian School – 1978

Catholic High Schools in St. Louis City

St. Alphonsus Liguori High School– 1920s
St. John the Baptist High School – 1922

St. Anthony High School – 1922
Nerinx Hall High School – 1924
Villa Duchesne School –1929
St. Mary's High School – 1947,
(founded in 1931as South Side High School)
Incarnate Word Academy – 1932
Notre Dame High School – 1934
St. Francis DeSales High School – 1939
DeAndreis Catholic High School – 1942
Bishop DuBourg High School – 1950
Laboure High School – 1942,
(founded in 1942 as North Side High School)
McBride High School – 1925,
(founded as Kenrick High School)
North Side Catholic High School – 1942
Cardinal Ritter High School – 1979
Augustinian Academy for Boys – 1961
St. Mark's the Evangelist High School – 1910

St. Louis City Historical Neighborhoods

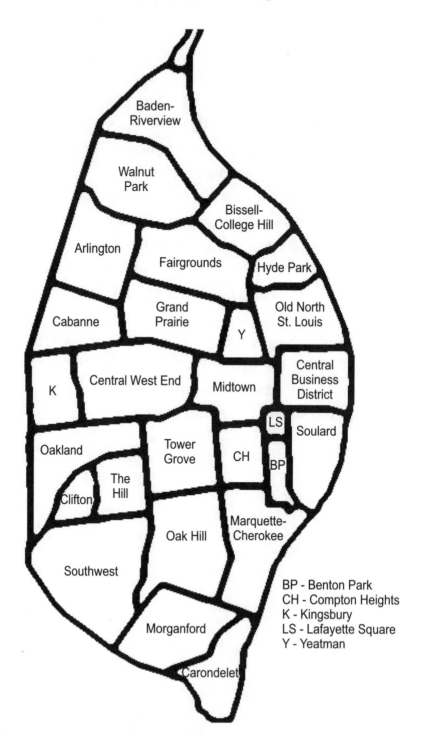

BP - Benton Park
CH - Compton Heights
K - Kingsbury
LS - Lafayette Square
Y - Yeatman

6 Chapter

Vocational High Schools: 1920 - 2004

St. Philomena's Technical School began in 1834 as an orphanage for girls of all ages. By 1845, the institution restricted admission to girls 14 and older and it became one of the first schools to provide a complete vocational program, teaching the skills of sewing and needlework. The need for vocational high schools was identified in the 1920s, and a vocational school program began in 1927. Hadley Vocational High School opened in 1931.

During World War II, Hadley Vocational, Ranken, and Booker T. Washington Technical School provided facilities for a "training within industry" program to teach courses on the aviation industry and generalized production skills.

The 1954, the United States Supreme Court's decision in the case of Brown *vs.* Board of Education had a significant impact on educational programs throughout the country. A year later, in 1955, the Supreme Court ruled that blacks were entitled to: 1) skilled teachers, 2) more high schools and 3) technical high schools. This ruling resulted in a second wave of vocational high schools and in the creation of specialized magnet schools in the City St. Louis.

In the 1960s, the St. Louis County Special School District (SSD), which had been founded in December 1957, moved into the area of technical education, a mission separate from the district's work in the special education field. SSD began providing technical education for the County in 1966 and opened the first public technical high school in St. Louis County in 1967. This new high school was named "South Technical High School."

St. Louis City Technical High Schools

St. Philomena's Technical School - 1834

Hadley Vocational/Technical High School - 1931

"Colored" Vocational High School – 1929

B. T. Washington Technical High School - 1934

O'Fallon Technical High School – 1956

Gateway Institute of Technology - 1992

St. Louis County Special School District Technical High Schools

South County Technical High School - 1967

North County Technical High School - 1968

West County Technical – 1982

7
Chapter

St. Louis-Area County High Schools

In 1876, St. Louis City separated from St. Louis County, and County residents began developing their own schools and school districts. Some St. Louis County high schools, such as St. Joseph Academy, Visitation and Ursuline Academy, were founded in St. Louis City in the early 1800s and, through a succession of moves, eventually became County high schools.

However, most of the County schools were founded when the great period of growth and expansion began after World War II. Soldiers returned home after the war, got married, and wanted a house for their families. They quickly discovered that there was a shortage of homes available in the City, but that in St. Louis County new homes were being built and sold for attractively low prices. Increased automobile production after the war and the start of the new Interstate highway system increased mobility and added to the great movement to the County. The expansion peaked in the 1950s, when a large segment of the St. Louis City population moved to the County. From the period of 1950 to 1970, the County population increased from 406,349 to 951,671, while the population of the City decreased from 856,796 to 622,236. By 1990, the population of St. Louis City was down to 396,685 and the population of St. Louis County was 993,529.

Some areas of the County began with single high schools. When the high school population increased, school districts were formed, and several high schools were built in adjacent areas to meet the demands. In other cases, school districts were merged, and a single high school, such as Maplewood-Richmond Heights, served the needs of multiple communities. And, finally, there were some areas where a single high school met the needs of the community.

Since the County didn't have a mass transportation system developed to the level of that in St. Louis City, the ubiquitous yellow school buses were introduced to transport students to and from school. In 1937-1938, the Normandy School District, one of the first to provide mass transportation for students, formed a transportation department and used taxicabs until buses could be purchased. Later, during school desegregation in the 1960s, buses were used to transport black students who lived in cities to and from schools in the suburbs, and a new term was created: "busing."

Some County high schools were named for their town, residents, or city, others after famous people, and still others after the area they served. A list of the 100 cities and towns that currently comprise St. Louis County is provided at the end of this chapter.

During this same period, the St. Louis County school districts consolidated from 93 school districts to 23 school districts. The current St. Louis County school districts are:

Affton
Bayless, Brentwood
Clayton
Ferguson-Florissant
Hancock Place, Hazelwood
Jennings
Kirkwood
Ladue, Lindbergh
Maplewood-Richmond Heights, McCluer, Mehlville
Normandy
Parkway
Ritenour, Riverview Gardens, Rockwood
University City
Valley Park
Webster Groves, Wellston

A brief summary of the current public St. Louis County school districts and their schools, as well as parochial schools and private schools, is provided in this chapter. The student enrollment provided for the County school districts is from the *Missouri School Directory 2001-2002.*

Affton School District

The Affton School District was established 1855. The District headquarters are located at 8701 Mackenzie in Affton. The 2001–2002 district enrollment was 2,627 students. The phone number is 314-638-8770, and the Website is http://www.affton.k12.mo.us/. The high schools are:

Affton High – 1930

W. F. Gaunt High School -1936

Bayless School District

The Bayless education program began in 1868, when a one-room schoolhouse was built on farmland donated by the Bayles brothers. Later, the land donated by the Bayles brothers became the central district for the schools in the district. The Bayless Consolidated School District, which was named in honor of the Bayles brothers, incorporated in 1878. The district headquarters are located at 4530 Weber Road in Bayless. The 2001–2002 district enrollment was 1,489 students. The phone number is 314-631-2244, and the Website is http://info.csd.org/schools/bayless/home. The high school is:

Bayless Senior High – 1935

Brentwood School District

The City of Brentwood was founded in 1919, and the Brentwood School District was established on March 3, 1920. The city was named after Mr. Brent, a local landowner, and presumably the woods on his property. Prior to the founding of the district, students attended school in Rock Hill. The School District headquarters are located at 90 Yorkshire Lane in Brentwood. The 2001–2002 district enrollment was 929 students. The Website is www.brentwood.K12.mo.us, and the phone number is 314-962-4507. The high school is:

Brentwood High 1927

Clayton School District

Clayton had its first meeting to discuss the construction of a one-room schoolhouse on March 5, 1880, and the school opened in the fall of 1880. The Clayton School District was established circa 1908, and district headquarters are located at #2 Mark Twain Circle in Clayton. The 2001–2002 district enrollment was 2,440 students. The District phone number is 314-854-6000, and the Website is http://www.clayton.k12. mo.us. The high school is:

Clayton High - 1917

Ferguson-Florissant School District

The Ferguson-Florissant School District was formed in 1952 through consolidation of the previous Ferguson and Florissant School Districts.

In 1902, Kinloch area residents voted to separate from the Ferguson School District. The new district became School District No. 5 until 1910, when it was renamed School District No. 18, Kinloch; it was also known as Kinloch School District. In 1936, the Kinloch School Board received approval from Work Progress Administration (WPA)* officials to build two high school buildings, one for blacks and the other for whites. A dispute over the location of the new black high school created a division between the residents of South Kinloch, the black area, and the residents of North Kinloch, the white area. As a result of the dispute, the Kinloch Board of Alderman approved the creation of the Berkeley School District on August 3, 1937.

*Works Progress Administration, a program of President Franklin Roosevelt's "New Deal" during the 1930s Depression.

The new Berkeley School District, made up of predominately white residents, began the 1937-1938 school year with one new high school and one elementary school.

On June 7, 1975, the Ferguson-Florissant School District was ordered by the U. S. District Court to annex an adjoining Berkeley District and Kinloch District.

The 2001–2002 district enrollment was 11,830 students. The communities served are Bel-Ridge, Berkeley, Calverton Park, Cool Valley, Dellwood, Ferguson, Florissant, Hazelwood, Kinloch and Normandy. The district headquarters are located at 1005 Waterford Drive in Florissant. The phone number is 314-506-9000, and the Website is http://www.fergflor.k12. mo.us/. The high schools are:

Central School – 1894
Ferguson High School -1939
Berkeley High School - 1937
McCluer High School - 1957
McCluer North High – 1971
Kinloch High School (white) - 1937
Kinloch High School (black) - 1938
John M. Vogt High School - 1930
McCluer South Berkeley High School – 2003

Hancock Place School District

Hancock Place School District was established in 1926. The district was named for Union General Winfield Scott Hancock (1824-1886), a hero of the Civil War. General Hancock's home was in Lemay. In 1890, he was a candidate for president of the United States. He lost to James A. Garfield by a narrow margin. Hancock died in 1886 and willed his farm to the Sisters of St. Joseph to establish a school and convent, but neither was ever built. In 1903, the first public school was erected at Gentry Avenue and Orient Avenue. The 2001–2002 district enrollment was 1,670 students. The District headquarters are located at 9101 South Broadway, and the phone number is 314-544-1300. The high schools are:

Hancock High School - 1919
Hancock Senior High - 1934

Hazelwood School District

The consolidated Hazelwood School District was established early in 1952. It was made up from the consolidation of 12 smaller school districts. The name comes from a farm once located near Lambert St. Louis International Airport, which had an unusual number of hazel bushes. Hazelwood traces its origin to the reorganization of Elm Grove School in 1949. In time, 12 more small districts joined the new Hazelwood School District, and the consolidation was completed in 1952. The district includes the communities of Hazelwood, Black Jack and Spanish Lake. It also includes a large section of Florissant, portions of the cities of Bridgeton, Bellefontaine Neighbors and Ferguson, as well as some unincorporated areas of St. Louis County. The communities served are Florissant, Hazelwood, Black Jack, Spanish Lake, Bridgeton, Bellefontaine Neighbors and Ferguson. The 2001 – 2002 district enrollment was 18,889 students. The headquarters are located at 15955 New Halls Ferry Road. The phone number is 314-953-5000, and the Website is http://www.hazelwoodschools.org/. The high schools are:

Hazelwood High School –mid-1950s
Hazelwood Central High School - 1976
Hazelwood East High School - 1976
Hazelwood West High School - 1975

Jennings School District

The Jennings School District was established in 1871, and the 2001–2002 district enrollment was 3,294 students. The district was named after James Jennings, a landowner who came from Virginia in 1839 and owned most of what is Jennings today. In 1960, the Jennings School District combined with the West Walnut Manor School District. The headquarters are located at 2559 Doorwood in Jennings. The phone number is 314-653-8000, and the Website is http://www.jenningk12.net. The high schools are:

Jennings High School - 1927
Fairview High School - 1926

Kirkwood School District

The Kirkwood School District, chartered in 1865, is among the oldest in St. Louis County, and one of the oldest west of the Mississippi River. The district covers an area of 15 square miles and serves Des Peres, Frontenac, Glendale, Huntleigh, Kirkwood, Oakland, Town and Country and Warson Woods. The 2001–2002 district enrollment was 5,061 students. The headquarters are located at 11289 Manchester Road in Kirkwood, and the phone number is 314-213-6100. The Website is http://www.kirkwood.k12.mo.us/. The high schools are:

Kirkwood High School - 1922
Kirkwood Senior High – 1955

Ladue School District

The Ladue School District was established in 1939, and the 2001–2002 district enrollment was 2,464 students. District headquarters are located at 9703 Conway Road in Ladue. The phone number is 314-994-7080, and the Website is http://www.ladue.k12.mo.us. The high school is:

Ladue Horton Watkins High – 1951

Lindbergh School District

The Lindbergh School District was formed in October 1949. The 2001–2002 district enrollment was 5,294 students and the headquarters are located at 4900 South Lindbergh Boulevard in Sunset Hills. The phone number is 314-729-2480, and the Website is http://www.lindbergh.k12.mo.us/. The high school is:

Lindbergh Senior High School –1950

Maplewood-Richmond Heights School District

Maplewood-Richmond Heights School District was formed in 1951 when the Maplewood School District consolidated with Richmond Heights School District. The 2001–2002 district enrollment was 1,083 students, and the district headquarters are located at 7539 Manchester Road in Maplewood. The phone number is 314-644-4400, and the Website is http://www.mrhsd.org. The high schools are:

Maplewood High School - 1930
Maplewood-Richmond Heights High - 1951

Mehlville School District

The Mehlville School District was established in the early 1900s. The district was named after Charles Mehl, who owned a farm on Lemay Ferry, and the nickname "ville" for village. The District currently serves an area of 44 square miles, including the communities of Lemay, Mehlville, Oakville and Concord. The 2001–2002 district enrollment was 12,056 students, and the headquarters are located at 3120 Lemay Ferry Road. The phone number is 314-467-5000, and the Website http://www.mehlvilleschooldistrict.com. The high schools are:

Oakville Senior High - 1974

Mehlville Senior High –1939, 1955

Normandy School District

The Normandy School District was established on July 12, 1894. It was known as District Number 2, Township 46, Range 6 East, Eden, St. Louis County, Missouri. The district headquarters are located at 3855 Lucas and Hunt Road in St. Louis. Communities served are Bellerive Acres, Bel-Nor, Bel-Ridge, Beverly Hills, Greendale, Glen Echo Park, Hanley Hills, Hillsdale, Normandy, Northwoods, Pine Lawn, Borwood Court, Uplands Park, Velda Village Hills, Vinita Park, Pagedale, Pasadena Park, Pasadena Hills, Vinita Terrace, Cool Valley, Charlack and St. John. The 2001–2002 district enrollment was 5,961 students. The school district phone number is 314-493-0400, and the Website is http:// normandy.k12.mo.us. The high schools are:

Washington High School - 1907
Normandy High School - 1923
Normandy Technical School - 1980

Parkway School District

The name "Parkway" was selected as the result of a contest. The district was named after Daniel Boone Parkway (also known as Highway 40 Parkway and as Interstate 64) because it ran through the heart of the district. Although it is one of the youngest St. Louis County school districts, Parkway Consolidated School District was established in 1954 by the consolidation of Fern Ridge, Mason Ridge, and Weber elementary school districts, which were founded during the 19th century. An earlier consolidation in 1951 had brought Barretts and Manchester Schools into the Mason Ridge C-2 District. Prior to the opening of Parkway high schools, elementary school graduates went to high school in Clayton,

Eureka, Maplewood, Ladue or private or parochial schools. Communities served by Parkway are Ballwin, Chesterfield, Creve Coeur, Des Peres, Manchester, Maryland Heights, Town and Country and Winchester. The 2001–2002 district enrollment was 20,231 students. The headquarters are located at 455 N. Woods Mill Road, and the phone number is 314-415-8100. The Website is http://www.pkwy.k12.mo.us. The high schools are:

Parkway Junior/Senior High School – 1957
Parkway Senior High School - 1961
Parkway Central High - 1968
Parkway West High – 1968
Parkway North High – 1971
Parkway South High – 1976
Fern Ridge High – 1992

Pattonville School District

The Pattonville School District was named after the community in which it was located. The community's name came from the Patton family, which owned a store on the corner of Fee Fee Road and St. Charles Rock Road. One of the Patton sons was the first postmaster in the area. The district headquarters are located at 11097 St. Charles Rock Road. Communities served by Pattonville are Bridgeton, Maryland Heights, St. Ann and unincorporated northwest St. Louis County. The 2001–2002 district enrollment was 6,464 students. The phone number is 314-213-8500, and the Website is http://www.psdr3.org/. The high schools are:

Pattonville High School - 1935
Pattonville Senior High- 1971

Ritenour School District

The Ritenour School District traces its roots to 1846,

when Buck School, a one-room log cabin, was built near the intersection of Woodson and Lackland roads on two acres of land donated by Mrs. Elizabeth Smith. In 1867, shortly after the Civil War, Buck School and a temporary school for Negro children were combined to form the rural district of Ritenour. The first recorded meeting of the Ritenour Board of Directors was Tuesday, April 2, 1878. The district was named in honor of J. S. Ritenour, a prominent landowner whose family owned a large tract of land in the vicinity of Lackland and Brown Roads in an area that was known as "Ritenour Hill."

The district headquarters are located at 2420 Woodson Road in St. Louis County. Communities served by Ritenour are Overland, St. Ann, St. John, Charlack, Edmundson, Vinita Park, Sycamore Hills, Woodson Terrace and Breckenridge Hills. The 2001–2002 district enrollment was 6,590 students. The phone number is 314-493-6010, and the Website is http://www.ritenour.k12.mo.us/. The high schools are:

Ritenour High School -1924
Ritenour High School - 1950

Riverview Gardens School District

Riverview Gardens was established in 1926. Prior to that time, the district was known as "Science Hill School District No. 7." The first high school opened in 1927 in the old Science Hill School, which was built in 1926. Communities served are Moline Acres, Bellefontaine Neighbors, Village of Riverview, Dellwood, Ferguson, Glasgow Village, Castlepoint, Hathaway Manor and Capital Hill. The 2001–2002 district enrollment was 7,587 students. The district headquarters are located at 1370 Northumberland in St. Louis County. The phone number is 314-869-2505, and the Website is http://www.rgsd.org/. The high schools are:

Riverview Gardens High School - 1927
Riverview Gardens Senior High School - 1957

Rockwood School District

In 1949, the R-6 district was organized from 21 small districts. In April 1964, the R-6 School District became the Rockwood School District. The headquarters are located at 111 East North Street in Eureka. The district services portions of the following communities: Ballwin, Chesterfield, Clarkson Valley, Ellisville, Eureka, Fenton, Manchester, Wildwood and Winchester. The 2001–2002 district enrollment was 21,547 students. The phone number is 636-938-2200, and the Website is http://www.rockwood.k12.mo.us/. The high schools are:

Eureka High School - 1934
Eureka Senior High - 1973
Lafayette High School 1960
Lafayette Senior High School – 1989
Marquette Senior High School - 1993
Rockwood Summit Senior High School - 1994

University City School District

The University City School District was chartered February 21, 1911. The 2001–2002 district enrollment was 4,291 students. The district headquarters are located at 8346 Delcrest Drive in University City. The phone number is 314-290-4000, and the Website is http://www.ucityschools.org/. The high school is:

University City Senior High - 1930

Valley Park School District

The first Valley Park elementary building, Hill School, opened in 1882. The school was located several blocks north of the present campus and was closed in 1931. The School District encompasses 4.6 square miles; enrollment in 2001–2002 was 1,064 students. The district headquarters are located at One Main Street in Valley Park. The phone number is 636-923-3500, and the Website is http://www.vp.k12.mo.us/. The high school is:

Valley Park High School - 1932

Webster Groves School District

The Webster Groves School District was established in 1868. The first public school began in leased quarters of the Old Congregational Church on October 11, 1869, and served both black and white elementary school students. Other school districts that joined the Webster Groves School District were the Old Orchard School District in 1901 and the Rock Hill School District in 1948. The 2001–2002 district enrollment was 3,540 students. The headquarters are located at 400 East Lockwood in Webster Groves. The phone number is 314-961-1233, and the Website is http://www.webster.k12.mo.us. The high schools are:

Webster Groves High School – 1906, 1924
Douglass High School 1925-1954

Wellston School District

The Wellston School District was established in 1896. Wellston and the Wellston School District are named for Erastus Wells. He was a St. Louis transit magnate who purchased a 66-acre tract of land in the area from the Kienlen family in 1868. Wells developed a country estate on the north side of St. Charles Road (now Martin Luther King) in a move to provide access to the area and aid its development. In 1878, Wells and others constructed the West End Narrow Gauge Railway that crossed St. Charles Road near Wells's estate.

Wellston Station was established there and became the nucleus for the Wellston loop and shopping district. Wells died in 1893. Later that same year, his home burned down; the estate became a subdivision. The 2001–2002 district enrollment was 692 students. The district headquarters are located at 6574 St. Louis Avenue in St. Louis, 63121. The phone number is 314-290-7900, and the Website is http://www.wellston.k12. mo.us/. The high schools are:

Wellston High School – 1923

Milliard Haulter High School - 1962

Eskridge High School – 1978

Special School District of St. Louis County

The St. Louis County Special School District (SSD) was established in December 1957, when St. Louis County voters passed a referendum to establish a local public school district to support the educational needs of children with disabilities. The district began in 1958 with four teachers and 166 students. The district headquarters are located at 12110 Clayton Road in Town and Country. The phone number is 314-989-8100. In the beginning, the students were taught in schools owned and operated by other school districts in the area. In a short time, SSD began building several special education schools. The first school was named "Ackerman School;" it opened in Florissant in 1961. In the 1960s, SSD moved into the area of technical education and opened three technical high schools: South Technical High School, North Technical High School and West Technical High School. (Details on technical schools are provided in the chapter about Vocational Schools, and the special schools are discussed in the special schools chapter.)

St. Louis County Catholic High Schools

The Catholic high schools have a long heritage in St. Louis

City and a relatively long heritage in St. Louis County. This chapter includes the early Catholic high schools as well as those that are the more recent arrivals to St. Louis County. The Catholic high schools are grouped into Archdiocesan High Schools, Regional High Schools, Parish High Schools, and Private High Schools.

St. Louis County Archdiocesan Catholic High Schools

John F. Kennedy High School - 1968
Mercy High School - 1948
St. Thomas Aquinas High School - 1954
Rosary High School – 1961
St. Joseph High School (for blacks) - 1937
St. Thomas Aquinas Mercy High School – 1985
Trinity High School – 2003

St. Louis County Parish Catholic High Schools

Coyle High School – 1939
Corpus Christi High School - 1957

St. Louis County Private Catholic High Schools

Chaminade College Preparatory School – 1910
Christian Brothers College High School – 1850
Cor Jesu Academy High School – 1956
DeSmet Jesuit High School - 1967
Gateway Academy of Chesterfield – 1992
Incarnate Word Academy -1932
Nerinx Hall High School - 1924
Notre Dame High School - 1934
St. John Vianney High School – 1960
St. Joseph's Academy – 1954 (founded 1840)
St. Louis Priory School – 1973
Ursuline Academy – 1926 (founded 1848)

Villa Duchesne School - 1929
Visitation Academy – 1962 (founded 1833)

County Regional Catholic High School
Duchesne High School – 1956
(founded 1924 as St. Peter's Parish High School)

St. Louis County Lutheran High Schools
The Lutheran high schools began in St. Louis City and then moved to St. Louis County.

Lutheran High School - 1946
Lutheran Central High School - 1946
Lutheran South High School – 1957
Lutheran North High School – 1965

St. Louis County Private and Other Parochial High Schools
Some of these high schools began in St. Louis City and then moved to St. Louis County, while others were founded in St. Louis County.

St. Louis Country Day School - 1917
John Burroughs School - 1923
Mary Institute – 1969 (founded 1859)
Mary Institute Country Day School (MICDS) – 1993
Westminster Christian Academy - 1976
Whitfield School - 1952
Thomas Jefferson School - 1946
Block Yeshiva High School – 1977
Logos School – 1970
Crossroads School - 1974
Chesterfield Day School - 1999
Christian Academy of Greater St. Louis - 1975
The Churchill School - 1978
North County Christian School

Nearby High Schools

The following area high schools represent a few of the many schools located in adjoining Missouri and Illinois counties.

Assumption High School (East St. Louis) – 1953
St. Theresa Academy (East St. Louis) – 1894
Rock High School (East St. Louis) – 1895
(*see* East St. Louis High School)
St. Charles High School (St. Charles) – 1922 (founded 1901)
Franklin High School (St. Charles) – 1921
Lincoln High School (East St. Louis) – 1908
East St. Louis Senior High School (East St. Louis) – 1915
Central Catholic High School (East St. Louis) – 1929
(*see* Assumption High School)
Northwest High School (Jefferson County) - 1950s estimated
St. Charles West High School (St. Charles) – 1970s estimated

Towns and Cities in St. Louis County
Affton
Ballwin, Bel-Nor, Bel-Ridge, Bella Villa, Bellefontaine Neighbors, Bellerive, Berkeley, Beverly Hills, Black Jack, Breckenridge Hills, Brentwood, Bridgeton, Calverton Park, Castle Point, Champ, Charlack, Chesterfield, Clarkson Valley, Clayton, Concord, Cool Valley, Country Club Hills, Country Life Acres, Crestwood, Creve Coeur, Crystal Lake Park, Dellwood, Des Peres, Edmundson, Ellisville, Eureka, Fenton, Ferguson, Flordell Hills, Florissant, Frontenac, Glasgow Village, Glen Echo Park, Glendale, Grantwood Village, Green Park, Greendale, Hanley Hills, Hazelwood, Hillsdale, Huntleigh, Jennings,

Kinloch, Kirkwood,
Ladue, Lakeshire, Lemay,
Mackenzie, Manchester, Maplewood, Marlborough,
Maryland Heights, Mehlville, Moline Acres,
Normandy, Northwoods, Norwood Court,
Oakland, Oakville, Olivette, Overland,
Pacific, Pagedale, Pasadena Hills, Pasadena Park, Pine Lawn,
Richmond Heights, Riverview, Rock Hill,
Sappington, Shrewsbury, Spanish Lake, St. Ann, St. George,
St. John, Sunset Hills, Sycamore Hills,
Times Beach (disincorporated in 1985), Town and Country,
Twin Oaks,
University City, Uplands Park,
Valley Park, Velda City, Velda Village Hills, Vinita Park,
Vinita Terrace,
Warson Woods, Webster Groves, Wellston, Westwood,
Wilbur Park, Wildwood, Winchester, Woodson Terrace

8

Chapter

Impact of Civil Rights and Desegregation on High Schools: 1955 - 2004

The Civil Rights movement reached its peak in the 1950s and 1960s. Activities such as organized gatherings, radio and television programs and news broadcasts, articles, pamphlets, books, parades, boycotts, demonstrations, marches, speeches, etc., laid the issues before the public. The demonstrations were an outward manifestation of the problems that had existed before the Missouri Constitution guaranteed education for blacks nearly 100 years before. During this turbulent period, St. Louis City's racial demographics went through dramatic changes. St. Louis's 1940 total population stood at 816,048, with 13% black, then increased to 856,796, with 18% black in 1950. In 1960, the population decreased to 750,026, with 29% black; then to 622,236, with 41% black, in 1970; and to 453,085, with 46% black, in 1980. By 1990, the population of St. Louis had decreased to 396,685, with 47% black.

The establishment of educational equality was at the heart of many problems. In the South, the concept surfaced with the integration of the blacks into white high schools. In the North, it occurred with equal rights, magnet schools, busing, and the renaming of high schools.

In 1847, the Missouri Legislature passed a law that prohibited blacks from learning to read, write, or assemble in public. John Berry Meachum (1789-1854) was a skilled carpenter and a former slave. He used earnings from his carpentry work to purchase slaves and train them, and then gave them their freedom. He also attempted to organize a school for black children, but the authorities prevented him from doing so. However, he found a legal way to work around the law. Since the federal government, and not the state of Missouri, controlled the Mississippi River, he built a steamboat and anchored it in the middle of the river. The boat was named "John Berry Meachum School for Freedom" and it was used to educate young black children in those turbulent years. Students were ferried in rowboats from the riverbank to the riverboat school so that they could attend classes.

When the Civil War ended in 1865, the restructured Missouri State constitution legally required education for blacks. By 1866, the St. Louis City census listed a population of 204,000, with 14,556 students enrolled in public schools.

Immediately following the Civil War, a number of constitutional amendments were proposed, but only three were passed. The three amendments ratified by the states to protect the newly freed blacks were the 13th, 14th and 15th Amendments. The 13th Amendment abolished slavery and involuntary servitude. The 14th amendment extended American citizenship to all persons born or naturalized in the United States and forbade any state to "deprive any person of life, liberty, or property without due process of law" or to deny any person "equal protection of the laws." And the 15th Amendment extended the right of suffrage to black men.

In the late 19th century, many states in the South created a racial caste system by passing statutes known as "Jim Crow" laws. "Daddy" Dan Rice, a white performer, introduced the name "Jim Crow" in the 1830s as a caricature of black entertainers in the white minstrel shows. In 1896, the U.S. Supreme Court legitimized the principle of "separate but equal" in its ruling Plessy *vs.* Ferguson. By 1914, every Southern state had passed laws that created two separate societies -- one black and the other white; this included separate schools.

In 1875, an abandoned white elementary school was selected for the first black high school in St. Louis and was named "Sumner." For 40 years, Sumner was the only designated black high school in St. Louis City or St. Louis County; it was, in fact, the only public high school that blacks were permitted to attend.

Chronological History

The following is an abbreviated chronological history of some of the major activities involved with the education of black children in St. Louis City and St. Louis County in the 19th and 20th centuries. These events eventually led to the voluntary inter-district desegregation program in 1983.

• The Missouri Compromise was enacted in 1820, and Missouri was admitted to the Union as a slave state in 1821. As part of the compromise, every future state north of Missouri's southern border was to be admitted as a free state. In time, Missouri became surrounded by free states, except for those at its southern borders.

• In 1876, the City of St. Louis separated from the County, making it necessary to establish a new school district outside the limits of the City of St. Louis.

•   Until 1890, most black schools were identified by numbers rather than by names of people or locations.

• Webster Groves added a black high school department to Douglass School, a black elementary school, in 1915.

• In 1932, the St. Louis City School Board arranged for space in Vashon High School for vocational classes, and Vashon High School continued as a regular black high school.

•   On September 21, 1947, in a letter to all churches in the St. Louis Catholic Archdiocese, Cardinal Joseph E. Ritter reaffirmed a policy to racially integrate its Catholic schools. In his letter, he advised of "the equality of every soul before Almighty God" and threatened to excommunicate St. Louis Catholics who raised objections.

• In 1954, the United States Supreme Court's decision in "Brown *vs.* Board of Education" [of Topeka, Kansas] impacted educational programs throughout the country. In 1955, the Supreme Court ruled that providing separate schools for blacks and whites was unconstitutional ("separate is not equal") and further ruled that blacks were entitled to 1) skilled teachers; 2) more high schools; and 3) technical high schools.

•   The St. Louis school desegregation case was first filed February 18, 1972, and was styled "Liddell *vs.* Board of Education of the City of St. Louis."

•   On December 24, 1975, Judge James H. Meredith approved a "Consent Judgment and Decree" that required the Board of Education to take certain affirmative actions. On appeal, however, the Eighth Circuit, by a panel of three judges, ruled that the Consent Judgment was not a complete remedy and ordered the case to continue.

• In a trial that lasted from November 1977 to May 1978, Judge Meredith ruled in favor of the defendants, finding that they had not violated the Constitution.

• The case was appealed; and, in March 1980, the Eighth Circuit Court reversed and found that the State of Missouri and the Board of Education were liable for unconstitutional school segregation within the City of St. Louis. The Eighth Circuit further determined that blacks were entitled to: 1) skilled teachers; 2) more high schools; and 3) technical high schools.

• On May 21, 1980, the case was remanded to Judge Meredith, and he ordered an approved plan.

• In the summer of 1981, Judge William L. Hungate was assigned to the case.

• Instead of a trial, and with the encouragement of Judge Hungate, negotiations began in earnest in February, 1983. Prof. D. Bruce La Pierre of Washington University led the negotiations, assisted by Shulamith Simon, a court-appointed *amicus*. The agreement was signed on March 30, 1983.

• Under the terms of the court-approved agreement, black students in St. Louis City could voluntarily transfer to predominately white school districts in St. Louis County, and white County students could transfer to magnet schools in the City. Additionally, programs were established to improve the quality of education the City. The State, as a constitutional violator, was ordered to pay most of the cost, and the Liddell case remained pending, with the court continuing to monitor compliance.

• In 1999, the Liddell Case, which had started the voluntary busing of students between St. Louis City and St.

Louis County schools, ended with a further, final settlement agreement. A key catalyst for the final agreement was that the Missouri Legislature agreed to provide continuing funding for the voluntary transfer program, permitting new students to enter the program for at least 10 more years.

During the 20th century, the St. Louis County school districts consolidated from 93 school districts to 23 school districts. The current St. Louis County School Districts are: Affton, Bayless, Brentwood, Clayton, Hancock Place, Hazelwood, Jennings, Kirkwood, Ladue, Lindbergh, Maplewood-Richmond Heights, McCluer, Mehlville, Normandy, Pattonville, Parkway, Ritenour, Riverview Gardens, Rockwood, University City, Valley Park, Webster Groves and Wellston. In addition, the Special School District provides services for students with disabilities and provides vocational education throughout St. Louis County.

Throughout this tumultuous time period, the St. Louis City and County school boards created a number of alternative and magnet schools to meet the various needs of the students, community and court mandates.

As of this writing, regular St. Louis County school districts and the Special School District were still participating in the voluntary student transfer program.

The St. Louis City magnet high schools are:

Academy of Language and International
Studies –1985– 1993 (moved to Soldan)

Academy of Mathematics and Science – 1976-1992

Central-Visual and Performing Arts – 1984-present

Cleveland–Junior Naval Academy – 1984-present

Gateway Institute of Technology – 1992

Health Careers – 1980-1992

Mass Media Program – 1981-1989 (at McKinley)

Metro–Academic and Classical High
School – 1992-present

NJROTC Academy – 1981-1984 (at Kennard
Elementary School)

Public Safety and Junior NROTC – 1980-1981

Senior Classical Academy – 1981-1990 (at Soldan),
1990-1992 (at Roosevelt)

Soldan International Studies – 1993-present

South Grand Work Study – 1969-1979

Sumner-Multimedia Electronic Graphic Arts (MEGA)

The St. Louis City alternative high schools are:

Business, Management Continued Education, and Finance
Centers and Office – 1980 (closed)

Center for Management, Law and Public
Policy – 1986-1993 (closed)

Community Access Job Training – 1966

Continued Education – 1969 (renamed
"Meda P. Washington" in 1995)

Delmar High School – 1975-1980

Lincoln or Lincoln Opportunity – 1967-1977

Martin Luther King, Jr. – 1975-1980

Meda P. Washington – 1995-present
(formerly "Continued Education")

Opportunity – 1966-1967

Pruitt Alternative – 1976-1982
Rock Spring Alternative – 1976-1980
Tri-A Outreach Center I – 1984-1993
Tri-A Outreach Center II – 1994-2000

The new St. Louis City vocational high school is:

St. Louis Career Education Academy – 1996 – present
(as of September 2004, known as "Clyde C. Miller
Career Academy")

9
Chapter

Specialized Schools:
1800 - 2004

This chapter on specialized schools describes a unique group of educational facilities located in both St. Louis City and St. Louis County. These special institutions were founded to solve social problems or to satisfy specific needs that could not be accommodated by the traditional schools. The public institutions were founded by taxpayers in St. Louis City and St. Louis County, while others were founded by religious organizations and by private individuals.

Some of these institutions prepare students for high school, while others not only function as high schools, but, in many instances, provide homes for orphans, specialized training for the disabled, correctional education, or vocational training for religious careers. In some cases, the institutions provide elementary, high school and college-level education. This chapter describes some of these institutions but does not attempt to describe all of those founded for special needs.

From 1850 to 1870, the number of institutions for dependent children in the St. Louis more than doubled. The tremendous increase was caused by many reasons; among the most significant:

- A cholera epidemic in 1849 killed 7,000 people (10% of St. Louis's population).

- A conflagration in 1849 destroyed much of the riverfront and killed many, leaving a large number of orphans.

- In 1849, St. Louis was the center for outfitting caravans moving west, and children of some pioneers actually were abandoned.

- 1849 was the height of the great German immigration, and a large influx of Irish came in the mid-1840s. Immigrants faced daunting problems, including a high birth rate, impure water, foul sewage, poor garbage disposal, the lack of extended family and social alienation.

The orphan population continued to grow, and the number of institutions increased until 1925.

Rachel Stix was born in Cincinnati, Ohio, in 1866, and married Elias Michael (president of the Rice-Stix Dry Goods Company) in 1886. Rachel became involved in many social activities in St. Louis and was director of the St. Louis Public Library, director of Security National Bank, director of the St. Louis Children's Aid Society, and Chairman of the Jewish Day Nursery. In 1922, Mayor Henry Kiel appointed her to the St. Louis Public School Board, making her the Board's first woman officer. In September 1925, the St. Louis Board of Education established Michael School, the first St. Louis public school for crippled children, which was named after her husband and located at 4568 Forest Park Parkway at Euclid Avenue. Rachel was a great patroness of the school. Today, St. Louis City provides schooling for students with special needs at Gallaudet School, Gateway Michael Elementary/Middle School and Gateway Michael High School.

In December 1957, St. Louis County voters passed a referendum to establish a local public school district to support the educational needs of children with disabilities. The district, which became the Special School District (SSD), began in 1958 with four teachers and 166 students. In the beginning, the students were taught in schools owned and operated by other school districts in the area. In a short time, SSD began to build several special education schools. The first, named "Ackerman School," opened in Florissant in 1961. In the 1960s, SSD moved into the area of technical education and opened three technical high schools, known as "South," "North" and "West" Technical High Schools. [Details on these schools are provided in the chapter about Vocational Schools.] The Special School District of St. Louis County serves St. Louis County and portions of Jefferson County covered by the Rockwood School District. The district headquarters are located at 12110 Clayton Road and the phone number is 314-989-8100. The Website is http://www.ssd.k12.mo.us/

In 1975, the "Education for All Handicapped Children Act" was passed. This eventually evolved into the "Individuals with Disabilities Act" (IDEA), which mandated free and appropriate public education for all students, regardless of their disabilities. Today, SSD educates more than 27,000 students with disabilities at locations throughout St. Louis County, including 265 public schools; and approximately 2,000 area high school students attend the district's two remaining technical high schools.

On January 8, 2002, President George W. Bush signed legislation to guarantee "No Child Left Behind." For more information, see the Website http://www.ed.gov.nclb/landing. jhtml.

Children's Homes/Orphanages
Academy of the Sacred Heart, founded 1827
Christian Orphan's Home-1887
St. Louis Colored Orphan's Home-1888
Protestant Children's Home, founded 1877 (as German-General Protestant Orphans Home)
St. Mary's Orphan Home-1900
St. Louis Christian Home 1923, founded 1887
Edgewood Children's Home, founded 1834
Epworth School for Girls-1864
Evangelical Children's Home, founded 1858
Missouri Baptist Children's Home, founded 1886
Mount Providence School for Boys-1933
Annie Malone Children's Home-1946
St. Vincent Home For Children-1950

Training Students with Disabilities
Ackerman School-1961
Bridge at Wirtz-1960s
Hiram Neuwoehner School-1971
Litzsinger School-1960s
St. Louis Vocational Special School
St. Mary's Special School for Exceptional Children-1953
Central School for the Deaf-1914
St. Joseph School for the Deaf-1837
Missouri School for the Blind, founded 1851
Southview School-1979
Gallaudet School-1901

Gateway Michael High School-1925
Gateway Michael Elementary/Middle School -1995
Turner Open Air School-1925
Northview High School-1964

In addition, the St. Louis Public School System has teachers at both St. Louis Children's Hospital and Cardinal Glennon Hospital to provide services to school-age children.

Bridges Program

The Bridges High School Program, located at 9375 Page Avenue in Overland, is operated by Special School District of St. Louis County for students with severe emotional problems. It accepts 7th- and 8th-grade students for all SSD school districts. The Bridges Program is a short-term placement for students from ages 13 to 21 years with challenging behavioral disorders. It provides traditional learning methods but also includes social skills training, conflict resolution and aggression replacement training. The curriculum provides high school credit for grades 9 through 12. The school phone number is 314-428-5234 and the Website is http://www.ssd. k12.mo.us/Sp_edu/Schools/bridges/index.html.

Correctional Training

Bellefontaine Farms (boys)
Delinquent Schools (previously operated by the St. Louis Public School District)
Griscom School
House of Detention for St. Louis Public Schools
Lakeside Center of St. Louis (now boys & girls) 1962
Meramec Hills (girls)
Missouri Hills (boys)

Religious Training

Carmelite Monastery, founded 1878
Concordia Seminary, founded 1888
Eden Seminary, founded 1858
Holy Family Seminary
Kenrick Seminary, founded 1818
St. Ferdinand Academy
St. Joseph Convent of Mercy
St. Stanislaus Seminary, founded 1823

Home Schooling and GED

Two unique approaches pertaining to secondary education are home schooling and General Education Development (GED).

• Home Schooling: The state of Missouri has statutory provisions that permit parents to educate their children at home. Details are available at Website http://dese.mo.gov/schoollaw/HomeSch/homeschool.htm

• GED Program; Each year, more than 10,000 Missouri residents earn their GEDs. The program allows people who did not finish high school but have knowledge and skills comparable to people who did graduate to earn a GED diploma. The GED consists of a battery of five multiple choice tests that cover high school material. Details are available at Website http://dese.mo.gov/divcareered/ged_index.htm

High Schools in the New Millennium

Overcrowding; underutilized facilities; growth limitations; stabilizing neighborhoods; the need to locate closer to the student population center; and replacing outdated and high-maintenance facilities: these are some of the reasons for creating new high schools and closing others.

Ittner-designed schools, such as Soldan, McKinley and Sumner, are still in use today. However, the grand Ittner architectural designs of the early 20th-century high schools are not being used for facilities built in the 21st century. The new schools are being developed with an eye toward quiet elegance, clarity, simplicity, practicality and economy. Post-Ittner high schools have many more constraints placed on them than their predecessors, but can draw upon past experience and can take advantage of the many new building materials and technologies available to them. Some of the reasons for the changes in architecture are:

- Handicap access
- Local and Federal laws and codes

- Air conditioning and heating
- Student parking facilities
- Security
- Computers and telecommunications
- Stricter fire and safety codes
- Changes in architectural preference
- New architectural materials
- Lack of building artisans
- Construction and maintenance cost limits

On May 30, 2003, the St. Louis City School Board hired Alvarez and Marsal, a business turnaround firm, to manage the St. Louis Public School System for an initial fee of $5,000,000 for a one-year contract. The Board retained the final vote on the firm's recommendations. On July 15, 2003, the St. Louis School Board voted to close 16 St. Louis City public schools. At the end of the 2004 school year, the management firm had completed its contract, and an acting superintendent appointed by the St. Louis Board of Education again managed the St. Louis School District.

Here are some recent examples of the new high schools just beginning or moving to a new location in the new millennium.

Vashon High School-2003
Cardinal Ritter College Preparatory High School-2003
Christian Brothers College High School-2003
Trinity Catholic High School-2003
McCluer South-Berkeley High School-2003
Clyde C. Miller Career Academy (formerly St. Louis
Career Academy)-2004

Future High Schools

High schools in the future will see differences in transportation of students, greater use of the computer, more use of the Internet in sharing teaching experiences, less use of formal textbooks, and the ability to obtain Internet computer information during long-term illnesses. Some of today's high school students have their own personal laptop computers and, in time, all students probably will have them. The computers will replace traditional textbooks and will contain graphical and audio interactive teaching aids. The students' computers will be connected in the schools by secure wireless Local Area Networks (LANs). Homework and tests will be entered into each student's computer and provided to the instructor via the LAN, and the instructor's computer will be used to grade tests and homework as well as to record grades that will be sent to the school's master file.

Computers, complete with audio and full-color video, are being used in many of the traditional classes such as math, English, history, science, language, etc., to provide additional subject information, collaboration with teachers and students from other schools, and online research.

"Virtual high schools" offer opportunities and flexibility by providing students with a way to enroll and take online courses on a computer in school, at a library or at home. According to a September 12, 2003, *St. Louis Post-Dispatch* article, at least 14 states run virtual schools that are recognized by a state agency. Students participating in virtual high schools are able to take make-up classes or take advanced classes not available at their school, are no longer restricted from taking a class because of limited class size, and have flexibility to juggle high school education with sports, after-school activities, and jobs.

Will people in the future still be asking, "Where did you go to school?" In 2050 or 2100 the question may mean "In what country did you attend high school?" "What computer network did you participate in to get your education?" or "In what company did you perform your apprentice work?" It is hoped that the education and socialization process of the adolescent educational years will have improved and that discrimination will be just something that is discussed in history class.

Appendix

Public High Schools

Academy of Language and International Studies High School

Date Founded: 1985
Location: 3230 Hartford in St. Louis City
Site History: Roosevelt High School
School History: After the Academy of Language and International Studies closed in 1993, the program was absorbed by Soldan International Studies.
Grades: 9-12

Academy of Mathematics and Science High School

Date Founded: 1976
Location: 4275 Clarence
Site History: old DeAndreis Catholic High School building
School History: The Academy of Mathematics and Science opened in 1976 and was located in the old DeAndreis Catholic High School building on Kingshighway. In 1992, Gateway Institute of Technology absorbed the program.
Grades: 9-12

Ackerman School

Date Founded: 1961
Location: 1550 Derhake Road in Florissant
School History: Ackerman School is one of five special education schools operated by Special School District of St. Louis County. The school educates students with a range of disabilities from kindergarten through eighth grades. Traditional classroom learning activities are often supplemented with services ranging from physical therapy and occupational therapy to speech and language services.
Grades: K-8
Phone Number: 314-989-7200
Website: http://www.ssd.k12.mo.us/Spedu/Schools/ackerman/index.html

Affton High School (1st location)

Date Founded: 1930
Location: 8520 Mackenzie Road, Affton
School Namesake: originally after the school district, later after Walter F. Gaunt, a teaching principal of an elementary school, and later principal of the high school
School History: Affton High School began in 1930 when classes were first held in the basement of Mackenzie School. The first graduating class consisted of seven students in 1934. In 1936, the first section of Affton Senior High School was opened at 8520 Mackenzie Road; later the high school was renamed W. F. Gaunt High School. In 1941, another Affton Senior High School was opened at 8309 Mackenzie Road.

Grades: 9-12
Enrollment: approximately 200 students when it opened in 1936
Mascot: "Cougars"
School Colors: purple and gold
School Paper: "The Cougars' Tale"
School Yearbook: "Affton Pride"

Affton Senior High School (2nd location)

Date Founded: 1941
Location: 8309 Mackenzie Road, Affton
School Architecture: contemporary, single-story, all-brick high school
School Namesake: Affton School District
School History: Affton Senior High School opened in 1941.
Grades: 9-12
Current Enrollment: approximately 863 students
Mascot: "Cougars"
School Colors: purple and gold
School Paper: "The Cougars' Tale"
School Yearbook: "Affton Pride"
Phone Number: 314-636-6330
Website: http://www.affton.k12.mo.us/
Alumni: John Goodman, actor

Bayless High School (1st location)

Date Founded: 1935
Location: 4530 Weber Road
Architect: Marcel Boulicult
School Architecture: two-story, brick colonial with columns at entrance
Building Cost: $140,000 in 1935
School Namesake: Bayles brothers, a local family that donated land for the schools

School History: The first Bayless high school students attended Central elementary school at Weber Road; the first graduation was in 1932. The first high school building was built on the central campus on Weber Road and was completed in 1935. The high school was remodeled and opened as Bayless Junior High in 1993. Central elementary school was demolished; on the site now are a parking lot and a cell phone tower.
Grades: 9-12
Mascot: "Bronchos"
School Colors: green and gold
School Yearbook: "Oracle"

Bayless Senior High School (2nd location)

Date Founded: 1957
Location: 4530 Weber Road in Bayless
School Architecture: two-story, brick contemporary
School Namesake: Bayles brothers, a local family that donated land for the schools

School History: In the 1950s, the population in the Bayless School District was increasing. A new high school building with a larger gymnasium was built; it opened in 1957 next to the old high school.
Grades: 9-12
Current Enrollment: 455

Mascot: "Bronchos"
School Colors: green and gold
School Yearbook: "Oracle"
Phone Number: 314-544-6342
Website: http://info.csd.org/baylesshome

Beaumont High School

Date Founded: February 1926
Location: 3836 Natural Bridge Road
Land Cost: $212,000
Architect: Rockwell M. Milligan
Building Cost: $1,673,725
School Namesake: William Beaumont (1785-1835), surgeon
Site History: Fairgrounds Park Neighborhood
School History: Beaumont High School opened in Fairgrounds Park area in February 1926 as a public high school.
Grades: 9-12
Current Enrollment: 1423 students
Mascot: Bluejackets
School Colors: Royal blue and gold
School Paper: "Beaumont Speaks"
School Yearbook: "Caduceus" (staff used as a symbol of the medical profession; in honor of William Beaumont, a surgeon)
Phone Number: 314-533-2410
Website: http://www.slps.org/Schools/high_2.htm
Alumni: Bob Koch and Fred Kovar from the 1952 Hall of Fame St. Louis University basketball team; both were nationally known basketball players. Blanche Touhill; Chancellor Emeritus, University of Missouri, St. Louis; Earl Weaver, Major League Baseball manager

Benton School

Date Founded: In 1853, the first St. Louis public high school classes were held in Benton Elementary School, also known as Schoolhouse #3.
Location: East Side of Sixth Street between Locust Street and St. Charles Street
School Architecture: two-story, brick colonial
Building Cost: $10,635
School Namesake: Thomas Hart Benton (1882-1858), St. Louis resident and U. S. Senator
School History: Benton School was built in 1839. Initial high school enrollment was 43 students. Benton School was St. Louis's third public elementary school. The first public high school classes were held there in February 1853. The school was located in the downtown business district on the east side of Sixth Street between Locust Street and St. Charles. It was the first public high school west of the Mississippi River and probably the first coeducational high School in the United States.

The initial courses of study offered at Benton School were similar to today's high school classes. They were "Higher Arithmetic, English, Analysis and Composition, Plane and Spherical Trigonometry, Surveying including Navigating, Analytical Geometry, History of the United States, Algebra, Geometry, Natural Philosophy, Natural History, Mineralogy, Geology, Civil Engineering, Rhetoric, Mental Philosophy, the Constitution of the United States, German, French, and Latin." The property for Schoolhouse #3 was purchased in 1839, and the school was built at a cost of $10,635. The architect's fee was $300 and the school was opened in January 1842.

Grades: 9-12

Berkeley High School (1st location)

Date Founded: 1937
Location: 6033 Caroline
School Architecture: one-story, brick colonial design
School Namesake: named for Berkeley school district
School History: Kinloch High School opened in 1937 as a "white," coeducational high school. Prior to its opening, white Kinloch high school students attended high school in the Ferguson, Normandy and Ritenour Districts on a tuition basis. Funds for the school were provided under the federal Works Progress Administration (WPA). After the Kinloch School District was divided and the Berkeley School District was created in 1937, the school was renamed Berkeley High School. Later, a new Berkeley Senior High School opened a block away, at 8710 Walter Avenue. In 1955, the building on Caroline Avenue became Berkeley Middle School and later the Caroline Center. The building is now boarded up and vacant.
Grades: 9-12
Mascot: "Bulldog"
School Colors: blue and white

Berkeley High School (2nd location)

Date Founded: 1955
Location: 8710 Walter Avenue in Berkeley, near Lambert Airport
School Architecture: two-story, brick and glass contemporary design
School Namesake: named for Berkeley school district
School History: Berkeley High School opened in 1937 and was located at 6033 Caroline. Berkeley High School later relocated to a new facility a block away, at 8710  Walter Avenue in Berkeley. In 2004, the school closed, and the students transferred to the new McCluer South-Berkeley High School. Some of the funds for the new high school were paid at the expense of the Lambert-St. Louis Airport expansion. The building is vacant.
Grades: 9-12
Enrollment: 409 students in 2003
Mascot: "Bulldog"
School Colors: blue and white

Blewett High School

Date Founded: 1933
Location: 5351 Enright, St. Louis City
Architect: Mauran, Russell and Garden
School Architecture: Renaissance Revival, red brick, terra cotta and stone
Building Cost: $275,000 in 1905
School Namesake: Ben Blewett
Site History: Building purchased form Washington University in 1917 and housed Blewett Junior High School, Harris Teachers College, and Enright Middle School.
School History: Blewett High School opened in 1933. The building was purchased from Washington University in 1917 after Smith Academy and Manual Training School closed. The building also housed Blewett Junior High School, Harris Teachers College, and Enright Middle School. Ben Blewett High School existed from 1933 to 1948. In 1948, Blewett's students transferred to Soldan High School and combined with Soldan's student body to create Soldan-Blewett High School. The Blewett High School was one block east of Soldan on Enright. In 1955, the name of the school changed from

"Soldan-Blewett" back to "Soldan High School" until 1990. In 1993, the Soldan school building on Union reopened as a magnet school and was given its current name, "Soldan International Studies High School." In 1948, the Blewett High School facility at 5321 Enright was changed back to Enright Middle School. At this time the building still exists but is vacant.
Grades: 9-12

Booker T. Washington Technical High School

Date Founded: 1934 by renaming Franklin Elementary School, which was built in 1909
Location: 814 North 19th Street
School Architecture: All-brick, four-story building with 16 classrooms, 12 shop rooms, gym, showers, and 1,100-seat auditorium
Building Cost: $214,528; 1936 auto shop added for $23,528
School Namesake: Booker Taliaferro Washington (1856-1934), who was born as a slave in Franklin County, Virginia, and became a famous educator; established Tuskegee Institute
School History: Building was Franklin Elementary School built in 1909. The original high school name was "Colored" Vocational High School.
Grades: 9-12
Enrollment: 1,050 students in 1936
School Closing Date: 1956

Brentwood High School

Date Founded: 1927
Location: 2221 High School Drive, Brentwood
School Architecture: Colonial, two-story, brick building
School Namesake: Mr. Brent, a local landowner
Site History: farmland and woods
School History: Brentwood High School, located in the Brentwood School District, opened in 1927. In 1961, Brentwood Junior High School was constructed next to the high school on the same property. Later, the junior high school became Brentwood Middle School.

Grades: 9-12
Current Enrollment: approximately 275
Mascot: "Eagle"
School Colors: purple and gold
School Paper: "Eaglet"
School Yearbook: "Eagle"
Phone Number: 314-962-3837
Website: http://www.brentwood.k12.mo.us/
Alumni: Ivory Crockett, a world record-setting, 100-meter runner, attended Brentwood High School.

Bridge at Wirtz School

Date Founded: 1960s (estimated)
Location: 1832 Schuetz, St. Louis County
School History: Wirtz Elementary School used for Special School District Bridges Program. The school is closed.
Grades: 9-12 credit (ages 13-21)

Business, Management and Finance Centers and Office High School

Date Founded: 1980
Location: 814 N. 19th Street in St. Louis City
Site History: Franklin Elementary School
School History: Business, Management and Finance Centers and Office opened in 1980 in Franklin School at 814 N. 19th. The Center closed in 1986.
Grades: 9-12

Career Education Academy (St. Louis Career Academy)

Date Founded: 1996
Location: 3125 S. Kingshighway
School History: The Career Education Academy, later known as the "St. Louis Career Academy," is located at 3125 South Kingshighway in the old Southwest High School facility. In September 2004, it was renamed "Clyde C. Miller Career Academy," and the students moved to the new facility at 1000 North Grand Avenue.
Grades: 9-12
Mascot: "Phoenix"
School Colors: Navy blue and gold
School Motto: "Through these Halls Walk the Finest Students in St. Louis."

Center for Management, Law and Public Policy Education

Date Founded: 1986
Location: 814 N. 19th Street in St. Louis City
Site History: Franklin Elementary School
School History: The Center for Management, Law and Public Policy opened in 1986 and was located in the Franklin School building at 814 N. 19th. In 1993, the program ended and was absorbed by Soldan International Studies.
Grades: 9-12

Central High School (2nd location)

Date Founded: 1855
Location: Northwest corner of Olive and 15th Streets, St. Louis City
Land Cost: $15,000
Architect: William Rumbold
School Architecture: ornate, three-story, Gothic-Revival, all-brick building that contained 11 classrooms
Building Cost: $40,000
School Namesake: none. Originally called "High School," then named "Central High School."
Site History: A 150-foot by 106.5-foot lot was purchased for the school from James H. Lucas in January 1853. Part of the site is currently a parking lot.
School History: "High School," as it was called, opened in 1856. It was located at the Northwest corner of 15th and Olive Streets and superseded Benton School, the City high school. The new high school building was the first St. Louis public school built exclusively as a high school. In fact, its name was High School, and the school letter was "H." (Later, it was called "Central High School.") Construction began in 1855. In 1889, the school enrollment was 525 students. The building served as Central High School until 1893, when it was replaced by the new Central High School at 1020 N. Grand. The school at Olive and 15th Streets closed in 1893.
Grades: 9-12

School Paper: "The Nut," 1886, "The Reflector,"1891
Alumni: Leo Rassleur, Commander-in-Chief of the Grand Army of the Republic during the Civil War; Nathan Frank, U. S. congressman and Director of the St. Louis 1904 World's Fair

Central High School (3rd location)

Date Founded: 1893
Location: 1020 North Grand Avenue, St. Louis City
Land Cost: $34,000
Architect: Furlong and Brown, with Isaac Taylor as consulting architect
School Architecture: Romanesque-style, red brick with white stone trim; multi-peaked roof, curved front façade; 140-foot stone tower to the side of the main entrance housed the stairway
Building Cost: $364,846
School Namesake: named for central location
Site History: In April 1886, a lot 193 feet by 360 feet was purchased for the school. The site was later used for the first location for Hadley Vocational High School and then Vashon High School.
School History: The school opened in 1893 and was designed to accommodate 1,200 students. It was 135 feet wide by 282 feet deep, with a stone tower 140 feet high. The auditorium was 82 feet by 84 feet, and there was a grand central stairway that was designed to be a prominent architectural feature. The building was badly damaged by a tornado on September 29, 1927.
Grades: 9-12
School Colors: red and black
School Paper: "Central High School News;" and in 1896, "The High School News"
Alumni: Charles Nagel (1909-1912), founder of U. S. Chamber of Commerce and Secretary of Commerce and Labor (1909-1913); Fannie Hurst (1905), author; Edgar Monsanto Queeny (1913)

Central High School (4th location) (formerly Yeatman High School)

Date Founded: 1928
Location: 3616 North Garrison Avenue, St. Louis City
Land Cost: $35,000 in 1902
Architect: William B. Ittner; Isaac Taylor, consulting architect
School Architecture: Three-story, all-brick building with twin towers
Building Cost: $307,766 in 1903, exclusive of electrical wiring, heating, plumbing and furnishings
School Namesake: named for predecessor
School History: When it opened on September 1, 1893, "Central High School" became the name for the older public High School that had been at 15th and Olive Streets. The school was located at 1020 N. Grand at Finney. It was an ornate, four-story, all-brick, Victorian-style building with a multi-peaked roof, curved front façade, and large steeple structure housing the stairway on the right side, where the main entrance was located. On September 29, 1927, Central High School was almost entirely destroyed by a tornado. The school's students were transferred to Yeatman High School at 3616 N. Garrison, which was later renamed "Central High School." The remaining south wall of the severely damaged building at 1030 N. Grand was retained and used in construction of the new building, which became "Hadley Vocational High School" and, later, "Vashon High School."
Grades: 9-12
School Colors: red and black
Current Status: In 1984, Central High School became a magnet high school and was renamed "Central Visual and Performing Arts High School."
School Paper: "The News" in 1952
Alumni: David Merrick (1930), Tony award-winning Broadway producer; Freeman Bosley, Jr.; former mayor of St. Louis; Siegfried Reinhardt, artist

Central Institute for the Deaf

Date Founded: 1914
Location: 4560 Clayton Avenue
Site History: Central Institute for the Deaf was founded in 1914 to provide education for hearing-impaired children. The institute's facilities have been located at 818 South Euclid Avenue for the past 70 years; previously, it was at 800 South Kingshighway. The administration and research facility is at 4560 Clayton Avenue.
Grades: currently, birth to 12 years of age

Central School (Ferguson)

Date Founded: 1894
Location: 201 Wesley Avenue, Ferguson
Land Cost: $1,000 in 1877
School Architecture: Two-story, four-room, brick building with a steeple; built in 1880
Building Cost: $5,600
School History: Central High School opened as a two-year, "white," coeducational high school in 1894. In 1902, Ferguson School District separated from Kinloch District at the request of the Kinloch residents. In 1903, Central became the first four-year public high school in St. Louis County. In 1915, the Missouri State Department of Education ranked the high school as "first class" and granted a fully accredited membership in North Central Association for Colleges and Secondary Schools. The high school students were charged $40.00 tuition, and the primary students were charged $20.00. The black students traveled to Webster Groves to attend high school. The high school closed in 1930, when the students transferred to the new John M. Vogt High School on Church Street. The building is now used as an elementary school.
Grades: 9-12
Yearbook: "Miaketa" (1924-1926), named for the Oklahoma Indian chief who camped in the Ferguson area prior to appearing in the 1904 World's Fair.

Central Visual and Performing Arts High School (magnet high school)

Date Founded: 1984
Location: 3616 North Garrison
School Namesake: named for school program
School History: Previously Yeatman High School, Central High School, and then a magnet high school for visual and performing arts. In June 2004, the St. Louis School Board closed the visual and performing arts school, and students were transferred to the former Southwest High School on South Kingshighway Boulevard.
Grades: 9-12
Current Enrollment: approximately 721 students
Mascot: "Eagle"
School Colors: white (ecru) and gold
School Paper: "The Eagle"
School Yearbook: "The Golden Eagle"
Phone Number: 314-371-1045
Website: http://www.slps.k12.mo.us/Schools/high/central/index2.htmAlumni

Clayton High School (1st location)

Date Founded: 1908
Location: 7500 Maryland Avenue
Building Cost: $125,000
School Namesake: named for city of Clayton
Site History: In 1952, the original high school was sold to Famous-Barr Department Store for

$326,000. Later, the site was used as a parking lot for Famous-Barr.
School History: The first Clayton High School class met in 1908 in the upper floors of the Grammar School (later Forsythe School). The first graduation was on June 16, 1911, and consisted of nine students. Later, space was rented on the second floor at Luecke-Bopp Building on Central Avenue. The first Clayton High School was at 7500 Maryland Avenue in Clayton; it opened in September 1917. The all-brick, three-story building was constructed at a cost of $125,000.
Grades: 9-12

Clayton High School (2nd building)

Date Founded: 1952
Location: 1 Mark Twain Circle, Clayton
Architect: William Ittner, Inc.
School Architecture: contemporary
School Namesake: named for city of Clayton
School History: The coeducational public high school opened in 1952
Grades: 9-12
Current Enrollment: approximately 900 coeducational students
Mascot: "Greyhound"
School Colors: blue and orange
School Paper: "Globe"
School Yearbook: "Clamo"
Phone Number: 314-854-6600
Website: http://www.chs.clayton.k12.mo.us/

Cleveland High School

Date Founded: September 6, 1915
Location: 4352 Louisiana
Architect: William B. Ittner
School Architecture: Three-story, all-brick, Jacobean Revival "castle" structure
Building Cost: $737,047, including heating
School Namesake: named in honor of Grover Cleveland, the 22nd and 24th President of the United States (1885-1889 and 1893-1897)
Site History: Previously a vineyard owned by Phillip Bardenheier. The lot purchased for the high school was 341 feet on Grand Avenue, 1189 feet on Osceola and 353 feet on Virginia Avenue.
School History: Named "Southern High School" before it was changed to "Grover Cleveland." When the school opened in 1915, the enrollment was 1,254 students. Cleveland High School remained a neighborhood high school until 1984, when it became a magnet high school and was renamed "Cleveland Junior Naval Academy High School."
Grades: 9-12
Mascot: "Cleveland Dutchmen"
School Colors: orange and blue
School Paper: "Gleanings of Cleveland"
School Yearbook: "The Beacon"
Alumni: Mazie Krebs, the designer of the unique 1940 "Admiral" riverboat; Harry J. Keough, captain of the U. W. Olympic soccer team in 1952 and 1956; Lou Thesz, world wrestling champion

Cleveland Junior Naval Academy High School (magnet school)
Date Founded: Started in 1981
Location: 4352 Louisiana
Architect: William B. Ittner
School Architecture: Three-story, all-brick, Gothic-Tudor "castle" structure

School Namesake: Named in honor of Grover Cleveland, the 22nd and 24th President of the United States (1885-1889 and 1893-1897)
Site History: Previously a vineyard owned by Phillip Bardenheier; Cleveland High School
School History: Named "Southern High School" before it was changed to "Grover Cleveland." In 1984, the school became a magnet high school and was renamed "Cleveland Junior Naval Academy High School" (magnet high school). Cleveland Junior Naval Academy is sometimes referred to incorrectly as "NJROTC" (Naval Junior Reserved Officer Training Corps). The Junior Naval Academy was founded in St. Louis in 1981 in the Kennard School building at 5031 Potomac. This joint partnership between the St. Louis Public Schools and the United States Navy created the second largest American naval academy, after the U. S. Naval Academy at Annapolis. Cleveland Junior Naval Academy cadets are unique in that they wear their uniforms to school five days a week. This magnet school was created to support the voluntary desegregation program between St. Louis City and St. Louis County.
Grades: 9-12
Current Enrollment: 1,060 students
Mascot: "Commander"
School Colors: Navy blue and gold
School Yearbook: "Reflections of Cleveland NJROTC"; also the "Muster"
School Motto: "Put Children First"
Phone Number: 314-832-0933
Website: http:/www.slps.k12.mo.us/Schools/high/cleveland/Cleveland.htm

Clyde C. Miller Career Academy

Date Founded: August 29, 2004 (grand opening)
Location: 1000 Grand Avenue at Bell Avenue in St. Louis
Architect: Kennedy Associates
School Architecture: modern design of light-colored brick, with a pointed glass atrium at the entrance
Building Cost: $30,000,000
School Namesake: Clyde C. Miller, former Superintendent of Schools
Site History: old Vashon High School on Bell and Central High School on Grand

School History: In September 2004, Career Academy students transferred to the new school from the old Southwest High School facility.
Current Enrollment: approximately 800 students
Grades: 9-12

Colored Vocational High School (1st location)

Date Founded: 1929
Location: 23rd and Carr Streets
School History: First vocational school for African-American students. Classes held in old Carr Lane School until 1932, when it moved to the new location.
Grades: 9-12

Colored Vocational High School (2nd location)

Date Founded: 1932
Location: 3026 Laclede
School Namesake: Franklin Building named in honor of Benjamin Franklin (1706-1790), American statesman and philosopher.
Site History: Vashon High School
School History: In 1932, Colored Vocational High School students moved into the old Vashon High School building at this location. In 1934, the school was renamed "Booker T. Washington Vocational High School" and moved to the Franklin Building at 814 North 19th Street.
Grades: 9-12

Community Access Job Training

Date Founded: 1966
Location: 4915 Donovan
Site History: Former Southwest High School and then former Nottingham Elementary School
School History: Community Access Job Training Program
Community Access Job Training Academy was located at 3125 S. Kingshighway, in the old Southwest High School facility, until June 2003, when it moved to a new location in the Nottingham School. This is a special school for students with mental disabilities.
Grades: 9-12
Current Enrollment: 113
Mascot: "Longhorn"
School Colors: yellow and Kelly green
Phone Number: 314-481-4095
Website: http://locations.slps.org/location.cfm?RecordID=114&BGCOLOR=white

Continued Education High School Program (*see* Meda P. Washington Education Center)

Date Founded: 1969
Location: 814 North 19th Street, St. Louis City
School History: The Continued Education High School Program opened in 1969 for continued education of expectant mothers. The program was initially located in the Dumas School at 1409 N. 15th Street; in 1971, it moved to the Curtis Branch School at 2825 Howard Street. The program continued until 1972, when it moved to the Carr Lane School at 2308 Carr. In 1976, the program was moved into the Gratiot School building at 1615 Hampton; and, in 1993, into the Franklin School building, at 814 N. 19th Street. The Gratiot School building, named in honor of Charles Gratiot, husband of Victorie Chouteau, currently is used as the Record and Archive Center for the St. Louis School District.
The Continued Education program remained under that designation in the Franklin Elementary School until 1995, when its name was changed to "Meda P. Washington School."
Grades: 9-12

Delmar High School

Date Founded: 1975
Location: 5883 Delmar
Site History: Delmar Elementary School building
School History: Delmar High School opened in 1975 in the Delmar Elementary School building, at 5883 Delmar, as an alternative high school program, used for overflow during a period of high enrollment. The school was named for the street it was on, and the street name was derived from the first three letters of the states Delaware and Maryland. The school closed in 1980.
Grades: 9-12

Douglass High School

Date Founded: 1915
Location: Holland Avenue near the ravine in North Webster Groves
School Namesake: Name submitted by students. Frederick Douglass was born a slave in 1817. He later escaped and published an abolitionist newspaper for 17 years. He recruited Negro troops for the North and was the first Negro to attend the inauguration reception of an American President (Abraham Lincoln).
School History: After a succession of other elementary school locations dating back to 1866, Douglass School began in North Webster Groves in 1895. It was a two-room, frame school for black children attending first through eighth grades. In 1913, basement rooms were added for high school classes; in 1925, three rooms were added to create a high school department. By the fall of 1928, Douglass High School had a complete four-year high school curriculum. In 1946, a new Douglass

Elementary School was built. It provided facilities for black elementary and middle school students until 1956, when the schools were integrated. For black boys and girls of high school age, it was the only African-American High School in St. Louis County. Prior to its opening, black high school students from St. Louis County attended Sumner High School in "The Ville." Douglass High School closed in 1956, and its students began attending Webster Groves High School. In 1960, Webster Groves annexed North Webster; in 1983, Douglass High School was demolished and replaced by 41 apartments named "Douglass Manor Apartments."
Grades: 9-12

East St. Louis Sr. High School

Date Founded: 1915
Location: 4901 State Street in East St. Louis City
School Namesake: East St. Louis City
School History: East St. Louis's first public high school was located at 5th Street and then moved to Howe Institute. After a tornado destroyed the Institute, "Rock High School" was built in 1895; it was located at 10th Street and Summit Avenue. In 1905, Horace Mann School was built next to Rock High School; in 1915, Rock High School was enlarged and became East St. Louis High School, a public coed high school. Later, because of increased enrollment, the school moved to 10th Street and Ohio Avenue to serve as the high school for white students. In the fall of 1958, the school known as East St. Louis Senior High School moved to its current location at 4901 State Street.
Grades: 9-12
Enrollment: approximately 2,064 students
Mascot: "Flyerettes" for girls and "Flyers" for boys
Colors: orange and blue
Phone Number: 618-646-3700

Eureka High School

Date Founded: 1909
Location: *See* School History
School History: Eureka High School was organized in 1908 and was housed in the Opera House over the old drugstore. In 1909, a four-room high school building was built, and two years of high school were offered. A new high school building, built in 1934, was located in Ballwin. At that time, Ballwin's white students went to Eureka and the black students went to Webster High School. In 1954, the schools integrated, and R-6 school district reorganized in 1949. In 1964, when R-6 became the Rockwood School District, Eureka students were transferred to Lafayette High School.
Grades: 9-12

Eureka Senior High School

Date Founded: 1973
Location: 829 Highway 109 in the Rockwood School District in Eureka
School Namesake: named for the town of Eureka
School History: Eureka Senior High School was founded in 1973 as a public, coeducational high school.
Grades: 9-12
Current Enrollment: approximately 1,295 students
Mascot: "Wildcats"
School Colors: purple and gold
School Paper: "Bugle"
School Yearbook: "Eurekana"
Phone Number: 636-938-2400
Website: http://www.rockwood.k12.mo.us/eurekash

Fairview High School

Date Founded: 1926

Location: 7053 Emma Avenue, Jennings
Building Cost: $60,000 bond issue
Architect: Bonsack & Pearce (now Pearce Corporation)
School Namesake: located on a ridge top overlooking the heart of Jennings
Site History: land inherited by Martha Jennings Mead, daughter of James Jennings. The back of the school has a natural bowl, graded for a track and football field.
School History: Fairview High School began in 1926 in the Walnut Manor School District (1916-1960), and in 1960 became part of the Jennings School District. The Fairview High School building, at 7053 Emma Avenue, opened in 1932 closed in 1969; in 1970, the building became Fairview Junior High School.
Grades: 9-12
Mascot: 1930s-1957 "Bluejays"; 1958-1969 "Warriors"
School Colors: 1930s-1957 blue and white; 1958-1969 red, white and blue
School Paper: "Courier"
School Yearbook: "Bluejay;" 1958 "Chieftain"
Alumni: Dan Gray, St. Louis television newscaster

Ferguson High School

Date Founded: 1939
Location: 701 January Avenue, in Ferguson
School Architecture: two-story, all-brick, colonial-style building with peaked slate roof and two massive chimneys
School Namesake: named for the community
Site History: "Blizzard Hill,"15 acres that had been the ruins of the January Estate (reputed to be haunted), and later the City dump
School History: Ferguson High School opened in 1939 and was built with $1,500,000 provided by the WPA (Works Progress Administration). The school had a firing range in the basement for the NRA Club's target practice. In 1939, the high school students from John M. Vogt High School transferred to Ferguson High School. In 1952, the Ferguson and Florissant school districts merged. In 1962, Ferguson High School had its last graduating class. McCluer High School became the *alma mater* for Ferguson's future graduates.
Grades: 9-12
Enrollment: approximately 400 coeducational students in 1939
School Yearbook: "Crest"

Fern Ridge High School

Date Founded: 1992
Location: 13157 N. Olive Spur Road
Site History: previously Fern Ridge Elementary School
School History: Fern Ridge High School is an alternative, coeducational high school in the Parkway School District that began in 1992. It is located in a facility that was formerly the Fern Ridge Elementary School, 1950 to 1982. Fern Ridge is a non-traditional, alternative program of accelerated academic preparedness, counseling, and  parent involvement, focusing on the students as a whole person by placing equal importance on meeting educational and emotional needs.
Current Enrollment: approximately107 students
Mascot: "Mustang"
School Colors: green and white
School Motto: "Because It Matters"
Phone Number: 314-415-6900
Website: http://www.pkwy.k12.mo.us/schoolportal.cfm?schoolID=24

Franklin High School

Date Founded: 1921
Location: 716 North Third Street in St. Charles City
School History: The "Frenchtown" School, purchased in 1870 from St. Louis University, opened as Franklin School for white elementary grade students. In 1902, the school was converted to an elementary school for black students; and, by 1914, all of the black students in St. Charles were attending Franklin School. The school added two high school classes in 1921, and the first four-year graduation was held in 1933. Because there was no 12th grade prior to 1933, some black students attended Sumner High School in St. Louis to receive a four-year high school diploma; this required a daily trolley ride of 52 miles. Franklin High School continued to expand until the schools were racially integrated in 1954. The last graduation at Franklin High School was held June 2, 1955; later, the school housed many special programs. During the population boom in the 1950s and 1960s, there was an increasing need for more schools. So, from 1963 to 1971, Franklin School became a kindergarten center for the St. Charles School District. Later, the facility was used for the district's central receiving, maintenance and storage.
Grades: 9-12

Gallaudet School

Date Founded: 1901
Location: 1616 South Grand Avenue in St. Louis City
Architect: R. M. Milligan
School Namesake: Thomas Hopkins Gallaudet (1787-1871), American teacher of persons with speech and hearing impairments
Site History: Compton school, opened in 1868
School History: St. Louis Day School for the Deaf opened in 1878 with eight students. It developed into Gallaudet School, which opened in 1901 in the renamed Compton School on Henrietta Street between Arkansas and Illinois Avenues. In January 1927, the school moved to a new school building at 1616 South Grand Avenue in St. Louis City. The school provides special programs for students with hearing, language or health impairments, autism, mental retardation and/or developmental and educational disabilities.
Grades: preschool-12
School Enrollment: 47 students
Mascot: "Bison"
School Colors: blue and gold
School Paper: "The Gallaudet Gazette"
School Yearbook: "The Gallaudet"
Phone Number: 314-771-2894
Website: http://locations.slps.org/location.cfm?Record ID=472&BGCOLOR=white

Gateway Institute of Technology High School

Date Founded: 1992
Location: 5101 McRee, St. Louis City
School Namesake: St. Louis, Gateway to the West
Site History: The facility previously housed O'Fallon Technical High School from 1956-1991, and the Visual and Performing Arts High School from 1976-1978.
School History: Gateway Institute Of Technology is a magnet high school located in the facility that previously housed O'Fallon Technical High School. The Gateway building also provides space for Gateway Michael High School, which educates children with medical disabilities.

Grades: 9-12
Current Enrollment: 1,431 coeducational students in 2002
Mascot: "Jaguar"
School Colors: Columbia blue, black and white
School Paper: "Gateway Times" once per month
School Yearbook: "The Way"
Phone Number: 314-776-3300
Website: http://www.gatewaytech.net

Gateway Michael High School

Date Founded: 1925
Location: 5151 McRee, in Gateway Technical High School
Architect: R. M. Milligan
School Namesake: Elias Michael (1854-1913), St. Louis civic leader and member of the St. Louis Board of Education.
Site History: Gateway Institute of Technology High School
School History: Michael School opened September 1925 as a facility to educate and serve children with orthopedic disabilities. It was located at 4568 Forest Park Avenue in St. Louis City. In 1995, the school was closed, and the students were transferred to the Gateway Complex. This transfer created Gateway Michael High School, which provides special programs for high school students with medical disabilities. Gateway Michael Elementary/Middle School is located at 2 Gateway in St. Louis City. It provides special programs for elementary and middle school students with disabilities.
Grades: 9-12
Current Enrollment: 10 students in 2002
Mascot: "Mustang"
School Colors: Royal blue and white
Phone Number: 314-664-7076

Gateway Michael Elementary/Middle School

Date Founded: September 1995
Location: 2 Gateway, St. Louis City
School Namesake: Elias Michael (1854-1913), St. Louis civic leader and member of the St. Louis Board of Education
Site History: Gateway Institute of Technology High School
School History: Gateway Michael Elementary/Middle School is located at 2 Gateway in St. Louis City. It provides special programs for elementary and middle school students with medical disabilities.
Mascot: "Mustang"
School Colors: Royal blue and white
Phone Number: 314-241-0993
Website: http://locations.slps.org/location.cfm?Record ID=552&BGCOLOR=white

Hadley Vocational/Technical High School

Date Founded: 1931
Location: 3405 Bell
Architect: George W. Sanger
School Architecture: architectural style looked like a large industrial manufacturing plant; 128 rooms

School Cost: $1,665,919
School Namesake: Herbert Spencer Hadley (1872-1927), Governor of Missouri and Chancellor of Washington University
School History: Hadley Vocational High School began as a vocational program in 1927, in the old Central High annex at 3432 School Street. In 1928, the school moved to 2918 Dayton; it closed in 1929. On November 2, 1931, the school reopened in a new facility on Bell Avenue in the Yeatman Neighborhood, and was known as "Hadley Technical High School." The school was coeducational and offered classes in Auto Mechanics, Bookkeeping, Cafeteria-Tea Room, Cosmetology, Drafting, Electricity, General Clerical, Machine Shop, Printing, Radio-TV, Sewing, Stenography, Welding and Woodworking. In 1956, Hadley Technical High School closed; students transferred and equipment was moved to the new replacement school, named "John O'Fallon Technical High School." In 1963, the "Hadley" building became Vashon High School from 1963 until it closed in 2002. In August 2002, the Vashon students moved into a newly constructed, modern high school at 3055 Cass Avenue. The building at 3405 Bell, originally known as Hadley Vocational School, was demolished in August 2002.
Grades: 9-12
Enrollment: the school was designed to accommodate 2,500 students.
Mascot: "Hornet"
School Colors: red and gray
School Paper: "The Dynamo"
School Yearbook: "Flame and Steel"
Alumni: Mary Wickes, actress (also attended Beaumont and Yeatman)

Hancock High School

Date Founded: 1919
Location: Gentry Avenue in Hancock School District in Lemay
School Namesake: The school was named in honor of Union General Winfield Scott Hancock, a hero of the Civil War.
School History: Hancock High School opened in 1919 on Gentry Avenue, and the first graduating class in June 1923 consisted of one student. In the 1925-1926 school year, the school was divided into a junior high group and a senior high group. In 1934, the students moved to new Hancock High School. The original Hancock High School building on Gentry Avenue no longer exists.
Grades: 9-12
Mascot: "Tiger"
School Colors: Midnight blue and gold
School Paper: "Hancock Newsette"
School Yearbook: "Memento"

Hancock Senior High School

Date Founded: 1934
Location: 229 West Ripa Avenue in Lemay (formerly Luxemburg)
Architect: Bonsack and Pierce, Inc.
School Architecture: three-story brick with some ornamentation
School Namesake: The school was named in honor of Union General Winfield Scott Hancock, a hero of the Civil War.
School History: Hancock Place Senior High school opened in 1934 as a WPA (Work Progress Administration) project. The present senior high school is located at 229 W. Ripa Avenue in Lemay (formerly Luxemburg). The school color shades have varied through the years.
Grades: 9-12
Current Enrollment: approximately 226 female and 212 male students
Mascot: Tigers

School Colors: Navy blue and Las Vegas gold
School Paper: "Growler"
School Yearbook: "Hancock Place"
Phone Number: 314-544-1200
Website: http://www.hancock.k12.us.mo
Alumni: One of the school's more well-known alumni is the founder of Dobbs Auto Centers in St. Louis

Hazelwood High School

Date Founded: mid-1950s
Location: 1865 Dunn Road
School Namesake: Hazelwood School District, named after hazel bushes in the area
School History: Hazelwood High School's first graduating class received its diplomas in 1956. The building is now Kirby Junior High School.
Grades: 9-12

Hazelwood Central High School

Date Founded: 1976
Location: 15857 New Halls Ferry Road in Florissant
School Namesake: Hazelwood School District, named after hazel bushes in the area, and "Central" for the central location in the school district.
School History: Hazelwood Central High School is located in the Hazelwood High School. The high school was Hazelwood High School until it was renamed "Hazelwood Central" in 1976, when the other two district high schools were completed.
Grades: 9-12
Current Enrollment: 2,573 students
Mascot: "Hawk"
School Colors: black and gold
School Paper: "Hawk Talk"
School Yearbook: "Torch"
Phone Number: 314-953-5400
Website: http://www.hazelwoodschools.org/Central/Central.htm

Hazelwood East High School

Date Founded: 1976
Location: 11300 Dunn Road in Florissant
School Namesake: Hazelwood School District, named after hazel bushes in the area, and location in the district
School History: Hazelwood East High School opened in 1976.
Grades: 9-12
Current Enrollment: 1,946 students
Mascot: "Fighting Spartans"
School Colors: burgundy and gold
School Paper: "Spectrum"
School Yearbook: "Pegasus"
Distinguished Awards: Missouri Gold Star School
Phone Number: 314-953-5600
Website: http://www.hazelwoodschools.org/East/East.htm

Hazelwood West High School

Date Founded: 1975
Location: 1 Wildcat Lane in Florissant
School Namesake: Hazelwood School District, named
after hazel bushes in the area, and location in the district
School History: Hazelwood West High School opened
in 1969 as a three-year junior high school (called
"Howdershell Junior High School"). In 1975, the building
opened as a six-year facility.

Grades: 7-12
Current Enrollment: 1,693 students
Mascot: "Wildcats"
School Colors: red and black
School Paper: "Gazette"
School Yearbook: "Focus"
Phone Number: 314-953-5800
Website: http://www.hazelwoodschools.org/West/West.htm

Health Careers Program High School

Date Founded: 1980
Location: 1530 S. Grand Avenue, St. Louis City
School History: The Health Careers High School Program began in 1980 at 1530 S. Grand. The program continued until Gateway Institute of Technology absorbed it in 1992.
Grades: 9-12

Hiram Neuwoehner School

Date Founded: 1971
Location: 12112 Clayton Road in Town and Country
School Architecture: single-story, brick and glass, campus-style facility
School Namesake: Hiram Neuwoehner, SSD Board President, (1957-1970)
School History: Hiram Neuwoehner School is located at 12112 Clayton Road in Town and Country. It is one of five special education schools operated by Special School District of St. Louis County. The school educates students ages 14 to 21 with a range of disabilities. Traditional classroom learning activities often are supplemented with a wide range of significant supports, tailored to individual students. The students are further supported by a variety of related service providers, including registered nurses, occupational therapists, physical therapists, social workers, speech/language pathologists and internal service providers in areas of vision, hearing and mobility. The high school is part of the St. Louis County Special School District.
Grades: 9-12+ (ages 14 to 21 years)
Current Enrollment: 175 students
Mascot: "Tiger"
School Colors: black and gold
School Paper: none
School Yearbook: name changes
Phone Number: 314-989-8700
Website: http://www.ssd.k12.mo.us/Sp edu/Schools/neuwoehner/index.html

Jennings Senior High School

Date Founded: 1915
Location: 8840 Cozens in Jennings
Land Cost: In 1935, the Shannon-Cozens-Clifton site was purchased for the new Jennings elementary school at a cost of $7,500
School Architecture: single-story, campus-style facility
Building Cost: In 1940-1941, funded by a $25,000 bond issue and WPA labor/grant. In 1955-1956, part of a $242,000 bond issue was used to build the auditorium and the gym. The Home Economics Department and shop were built from a $302,000 bond issue.
School Namesake: James Jennings, landowner of most of what is the city of Jennings today
Site History: In 1940, a small lake was drained for the high school.
School History: Jennings High School was founded in 1915, and the first graduation was held in 1918. In 1927, the first Jennings High School building opened at 8831 Cozens Avenue in the Jennings School District . The building became Jennings Middle School in 1941, when the present High School at 8840 Cozens opened. In 1960, Jennings School District merged with the West Walnut Manor School District (Fairview High School). The combined Jennings/Fairview High School class held its first graduation in 1970.
Grades: 9-12
Current Enrollment: approximately 763 students
Mascot: "Bulldog" until 1970; now "Warriors"
School Colors: red and white
School Paper: "Growl;"1969 - 1970 "Tomahawk Tims"
School Yearbook: "Jen Echo"
Phone Number: 314-653-8100
Website: http://www.jenningsk12.net/jenningssenior.html

John M. Vogt High School

Date Founded: 1930
Location: 200 Church Avenue in Ferguson
School Architecture: two-story, all-brick, colonial architecture, with a peaked slate roof and massive chimneys
School Namesake: John M. Vogt, former school board member for 22 years
Site History: Open-air theater, donated by the Community Hall Association
School History: In 1930, "Central School" high school students transferred to the new J. M. Vogt High School, the first dedicated high school building to be built in Ferguson School District. In 1939, the student body of 400 students was transferred to the new Ferguson High School on January Avenue.
Grades: 9-12
Enrollment: approximately 400 students in 1939
Yearbook: "Crest" began in 1931

John O'Fallon Technical High School

Date Founded: 1956
Location: 5101 Northrup
Architect: F. Ray Leimkuehler
School Architecture: Five-story, multiple-wing, all-brick building with plentiful windows and a flat roof
Building Cost: The first unit, consisting of the main building and the E building, contained 350,000 square feet and was built for approximately $12.80 per square foot (or 82 cents per cubic foot).
School Namesake: John O'Fallon, a prominent St. Louis philanthropist and promoter of early railroad companies (1791-1885)
Site History: located on the south bank of the old Mill Creek, which formerly flowed into Chouteau's

Pond, O'Fallon Technical High School opened in 1956 at 5101 Northrup (location of mailbox) as a successor to the Hadley Technical School. The school actually was on McRee Avenue.

School History: On September 6, 1956, John O'Fallon Technical High School, a coeducational technical school, opened for registration; it was dedicated on October 5, 1956. Students from the closed Hadley Technical High School transferred to the new school, which originally was planned to duplicate Hadley. However, the advent of integration required a larger school, and the "Atomic Age" changed educational concepts to promote integration of technical educational with general education. The school was closed in 1992. It reopened later that same year as Gateway Institute of Technology, located at 5101 McRee Avenue, west of Kingshighway, in the Oakland neighborhood.

Grades: 9-12

Enrollment: In peak years, approximately 3,000 full-time students (3,500 including co-op students)

Mascot: "Hornet"

School Colors: red and gray

School Paper: "The Dynamo"

School Yearbook: "Flame and Steel"

Kinloch High School ("white" school)

Date Founded: 1937

Location: 6033 Caroline Avenue, Berkeley (originally Kinloch)

School Architecture: one-story, brick colonial

School Namesake: Kinloch, then Berkeley (named after the area)

School History: Kinloch High School opened in 1937 as a "white," coeducational high school. Prior to its opening, white Kinloch high school students attended high school in the Ferguson, Normandy and Ritenour Districts on a tuition basis. Funds for the school were provided under the federal Works Progress Administration (WPA). After the Kinloch School District was divided and the Berkeley School District was created in 1937, the school was renamed "Berkeley High School." Later, a new Berkeley Senior High School opened a block away, at 8710 Walter Avenue. The building on Caroline Avenue became Berkeley Middle School. On June 7, 1975, the Ferguson-Florissant School District was ordered by the U. S. District Court to annex an adjoining Berkeley District and Kinloch District. As a result of St. Louis-Lambert Airport expansion, Berkeley High School on Walter Avenue closed in December 2003. In January 2004, the students transferred to the new McCluer South Berkeley High School on Brotherton Lane. Both school buildings currently are vacant.

Grades: 9-12

Mascot: Enrollment: approximately 120 coeducational, white students in 1938

Kinloch High School ("black" school)

Date Founded: 1938

Location: Courtney Avenue and Witt Street, Kinloch

School History: Kinloch High School opened in 1938 as a "black," coeducational high school in the Kinloch School District. Prior to its opening, a few black students attended Sumner High School in St. Louis, but the vast majority went without a high school education because the Kinloch School District was unable to make tuition payments. Some black students reportedly gave Ferguson addresses in order to be eligible to attend Douglass High School for blacks in Webster Groves. In January 1936, a high school program began for black students in Dunbar Elementary School under the auspices of the WPA Emergency Education Program. Later, in 1936, the Kinloch School Board received approval from WPA officials to build two high school buildings, one for blacks and the other for whites. A dispute over the location of the new black high school created a division between the residents of South Kinloch, the black area, and the residents of North Kinloch, the white area. As a result of the dispute, the Kinloch Board of Aldermen approved the creation of the Berkeley School District on August 3, 1937. The new Berkeley School District, made up of predominately white residents, began the 1937-1938 school year with one new high school and one elementary school. Funds for the new black high school in the downsized Kinloch School District were provided under the federal Works Progress Administration (WPA). The new Kinloch High School opened in 1938 and was located at Courtney Avenue and Witt Street. In 1964, John F. Kennedy Middle School for

black students was built on adjacent land. On June 7, 1975, the Ferguson-Florissant School District was ordered by the U. S. District Court to annex an adjoining Berkeley District and Kinloch District. At the end of the 1975-1976 school year, Kinloch's two elementary schools, the middle school, and the senior high school ceased to be used for classroom purposes. Originally, senior high school students were assigned to McCluer North High School in Florissant, and the students in seventh and eighth grades transferred to either Cross Keys or Florissant Junior High Schools. Kinloch Senior High School later became a vocational training center for students throughout the district and later was destroyed by fire. The former John F. Kennedy Middle School is now Kinloch's Government Center and Police Department.
Grades: 9-12
Enrollment: approximately 200 coeducational black students in 1938

Kirkwood High School

Date Founded: 1866
Location: 700 South Kirkwood Road, Kirkwood
School History: Kirkwood High School and elementary students started attending school together in 1866 in a temporary building and then moved into the Jefferson Avenue School, built in 1869. In 1888, the Adams Avenue School opened and provided a two-year high school program, followed in 1896 by the first four-year high school program in St. Louis County. The first graduation class, in the spring of 1897, consisted of 10 students. In 1922, a new high school building was constructed at 700 South Kirkwood Road. It remained Kirkwood High School until the new school opened on Essex Avenue in 1955. The facility on Kirkwood Road is now Nipher Middle School.
Grades: 9-12

Kirkwood Senior High School

Date Founded: 1955
Location: 801 Essex Avenue in Kirkwood
School Architecture: brick, single- and two-story, contemporary, campus-style buildings
School Namesake: named for the city of Kirkwood
School History: Kirkwood Senior High School is located on a 47-acre, seven-building, college-style campus in Kirkwood.
Grades: 9-12
Current Enrollment: approximately 1,741 students
Mascot: "Pioneers"
School Colors: red and white
School Paper: "The Kirkwood Call"
School Yearbook: "Pioneer"
Phone Number: 314-213-6110
Website: http://www.kirkwood.k12.mo.us/parent_student
Alumni: Patricia McKissack, author of children's books; Bob Reim and Herb Jones, former Kirkwood mayors; Kathryn Grayson, actress; Frank Keck, baseball player; and Doug Vaughn, KMOX Radio sportscaster

Ladue Horton Watkins High School

Date Founded: 1952
Location: 1201 South Warson Road in Ladue
School Architecture: Two-story, all-brick colonial with peaked roof
School Namesake: Horton Watkins, a shoe executive and philanthropist
Site History: Mrs. Horton Watkins donated the 28-acre tract of land on South Warson Road as a memorial to her late husband.
School History: Prior to Ladue Horton Watkins High School's opening in September 1952, area

high school students attended high schools in Clayton, Kirkwood, University City and Webster Groves. The Ladue School Board paid tuition for the students. Ladue High School opened in 1952 with 550 students in grades 7 –12. Enrollment grew at an average rate of 175 students per year, until the school had 1,514 students in 1958. In 1959, East Ladue Junior High School opened and relieved the overcrowding.
Grades: 9-12
Current Enrollment: approximately 1,076 students
Mascot: "Rams"
School Colors: Royal blue and white
School Paper: "Panorama"
School Yearbook: "Rambler," "Crescendo"
Phone Number: 314-993-6447
Website: http://www.hsweb.ladue.k12.mo.us
Alumni: Roger Dierberg, co-owner of a major food market chain in St. Louis area

Lafayette High School

Date Founded: September 7, 1960
Location: 16025 Clayton Road, Ellisville
School Architecture: two-story, contemporary, brick and glass building
School History: Lafayette High School opened its doors on September 7, 1960, with 288 freshmen and sophomores. It was located on Clayton Road at the site of the current Crestview Middle School. Open fields surrounded the one small building that comprised the school campus.
The building's size and location dictated activities in those early years: gym classes were held in the cafeteria, with students dressing out in regular classrooms; football games were played on the baseball field; proms were held in the gym; and Eureka and Lafayette High Schools shared a yearbook. Lafayette seemed an appropriate name for the school, as it was built in an area in Ellisville known as "Lafayette." In April 1964, the R-6 school became the "Rockwood School District." The "Lancer Mascot" made its appearance in 1965, and the Class of 1967 donated the "Lancer Seal." Increased student population forced Lafayette High School to move to its present location in 1989.
Grades: 9-12
Enrollment: 288 freshmen and sophomores in 1960
Mascot: "Lancer"

Lafayette Senior High School

Date Founded: 1989
Location: 17050 Clayton Road, at the corner of Clayton Road and Highway 109 in St. Louis County
School Architecture: two-story, contemporary, brick and glass building
School Namesake: Lafayette area in Ellisville
School History: Lafayette Senior High School is a coeducational public high school in the Rockwood School  District. Increased student population forced Lafayette High School to move to its present location in 1989. The 53-acre campus at 17050 Clayton Road, at the intersection of Clayton Road and Highway 109, greeted 1,800 students its first year.
Grades: 9-12
Current Enrollment: approximately 2,063 students
Mascot: "Lancer"
School Colors: black and gold
School Paper: "Image"
School Yearbook: "The Legend"
Phone Number: 636-458-7200
Website: http://www.lafayettehighschool.org/

Lakeside Center of St. Louis County

Date Founded: 1962
Location: 13044 Marine Avenue, St. Louis County
School Architecture: single-story, campus-style facility
School Namesake: the facility is located near Creve Coeur Lake
Site History: Previously known as "Lakeside School for Boys"
School History: Lakeside is part of the St. Louis County Special School District; it began in 1962 as a residential treatment center for young men. In 1988, the center began admitting young women. The students are provided with Individual Education Plans (IEPs), are instructed at the center, and can receive high school credit for the classes they complete.
Grades: 9-12
Current Enrollment: the capacity is 61 residents
Phone Number: 314-434-4535
Website: http://www.co.st-louis.mo.us/dhs/lakeside.html

Lincoln High School

Date Founded: 1908
Location: 1211 Bond Avenue in East St. Louis City
School Namesake: Abraham Lincoln, 16th president of the U. S. (1861-1865)
School History: Lincoln High School was founded in 1908 as a public, coeducational high school for students living in East St. Louis; it was located at 1100 Broadway. In 1956, Lincoln High School was rebuilt at 1211 Bond Avenue. Recently, it was designated as Lincoln Middle School.
Grades: 9-12
Alumni: Jackie Joyner-Kersee, Olympic athlete & philanthropist

Lincoln High School/Lincoln Opportunity High School

Date Founded: 1967
Location: 5017 Washington Avenue
School Namesake: Abraham Lincoln, 16th president or the U. S. (1861-1865)
School History: The Lincoln High School or Lincoln Opportunity Program, which also was referred to as "Lincoln Opportunity and Metro Work-Study," opened in 1967 as an alternative program. It continued until 1977.
Grades: 9-12

Lindbergh Senior High School

Date Founded: September1950
Location: 4900 S. Lindbergh Road in South St. Louis County
School Architecture: single-story, brick and glass, campus-style facility
Building Cost: $218,200 original building, completed November 1, 1951
School Namesake: Charles A. Lindbergh, famous aviator
Site History: Sappington School
School History: Lindbergh School District's first high school was originally housed in the basement of Sappington School in September 1950, and was called "Grandview High School." The school board purchased 40 acres of land and, on November 1, 1951, the first wing of the high school was completed. It consisted of nine classrooms, a cafeteria, kitchen, and offices. In April 1952, the name was changed to Lindbergh High School. The first graduation took place on May 23, 1954.
Grades: 9-12
Current Enrollment: approximately 1,819 students
Mascot: "Flyers"
School Colors: green and gold
School Paper: "Pilot"
School Yearbook: "Spirit"
Phone Number: 314-729-2410
Website: http://www.lindbergh.k12.mo.us/lhs/

Litzsinger School

Date Founded: 1960s
Location: 10094 Litzsinger Road
School History: Litzsinger School is one of five special education schools operated by Special School District of St. Louis County. The school educates students with a range of disabilities. Traditional classroom learning activities often are supplemented with physical therapy, occupational therapy, and speech/language services.
Grades: Preschool to eighth grade
Students: approximately 150
Mascot: "Lion"
School Colors: yellow and white
School Paper: none
School Yearbook: none
Phone Number: 314-989-8800
Website: http://www.ssd.k12.mo.us/Sp_edu/Schools/litzinger/index.html

Maplewood-Richmond Heights High School

Date Founded: 1930
Location: 7539 Manchester Road in Maplewood
Architect: William B. Ittner
School Architecture: three-story, red brick building with stone trim at the foundation and brick ornamental trim
School Namesake: named for the communities it serves
School History: In 1909, the Maplewood School District became one of the first districts in St. Louis County to offer a High School program. The land for Maplewood High School was purchased in 1925, and the school opened in 1930. In 1951, the Maplewood School District consolidated with the Richmond Heights School District, and the combined district became the School District of Maplewood-Richmond Heights. The high school then became Maplewood-Richmond Heights High School.
Grades: 9-12
Current Enrollment: approximately 132 female and 131 male students
Mascot: "Blue Devils;" basketball team "Leafs"
School Colors: blue and white
School Paper: "The Chip"
Phone Number: 314-644-4401
Website: http://www.mrhsd.org/about_schools.html
Alumni: Paul Christman, former Chicago Bears football player and announcer; Mark Christman, baseball player for St. Louis Browns; King Parsons, professional wrestler, a.k.a. "the Ice Man;" Robert Ulrich, Kansas City federal judge

Marquette Senior High School

Date Founded: August 1993
Location: 2351 Clarkson Road in Chesterfield
School Architecture: two-story, contemporary, brick and glass building
School Namesake: Selected by a committee of parents
School History: Marquette Senior High School opened its doors to 9th- and 10th-grade students in the Rockwood School District in August 1993, and is now a senior high school.
Grades: 9-12
Current Enrollment: approximately 2,046 students

Mascot: "Mustang"
School Colors: Navy blue and Kelly green
School Paper: "Messenger"
School Yearbook: "Medallion"
Phone Number: 636-537-4300
Website: http://www.rockwood.k12.mo.us/marquette/
Alumni: Whitney Weeks, Miss Missouri 2004

Martin Luther King, Jr., High School

Date Founded: 1975
Location: 1909 N. Kingshighway in St. Louis City
School Namesake: Martin Luther King, Jr. (1929-1968), clergyman and civil rights leader
Site History: former McBride Catholic High School
School History: Martin Luther King, Jr., High School opened in 1975 in the old McBride Catholic High School at as an "alternative" program for high school students. The school closed in 1980 and then opened as a middle school from 1980-1993.
Grades: 9-12

Mass Media High School Program

Date Founded: 1981
Location: 2156 Russell in St. Louis City
Site History: formerly McKinley High School
School Architecture: ornate, three-story, brick building with twin towers resembling an English castle
School Namesake: named for the programs taught at the school
School History: The Mass Media High School Program began in 1981 and was located in McKinley High School building at 2156 Russell. The program continued until 1989, when the Central Visual and Performing Arts High School (formerly Yeatman and Central High School) absorbed the program.
Grades: 9-12

McCluer High School

Date Founded: 1957
Location: 1896 South New Florissant Road in Florissant
School Architecture: two-story, brick contemporary
School Namesake: Virgil C. McCluer, school superintendent for 30 years
School History: McCluer High School opened in the 1957-1958 school year as a junior high school and became a high school in the 1962-1963 school year. After Ferguson High School closed in 1962, students were transferred to McCluer. The high school is located in the Ferguson-Florissant School District.
Grades: 9-12
Current Enrollment: approximately 1,600 students
Mascot: "Comets"
School Colors: red and true blue
School Paper: "Scoop"
School Yearbook: "Crest" (new name each year)
Phone Number: 314-506-9400
Website: http://www.fergflor.k12.mo.us/MC.index.html
Alumni: Michael McDonald, singer and songwriter

McCluer North High School

Date Founded: 1971
Location: 705 Waterford Drive, Florissant
School Architecture: Three-level, brick structure of 257,325 square feet and with 75 classrooms
School Namesake: Virgil C. McCluer, school superintendent for 30 years
Site History: McCluer North High School is located in the Ferguson-Florissant School District.
School History: McCluer North High School
Grades: 9-12
Current Enrollment: approximately 1,307 students
Mascot: "Stars"
School Colors: silver and blue
School Paper: "Star Gazer"
School Yearbook: "Polaris"
Distinguished Awards: Blue Ribbon School by the United States Department of Education, and Missouri Gold Star School.
Phone Number: 314-506-9200
Website: http://www.fergflor.k12.mo.us/MN.index.html

McCluer South Berkeley High School

Date Founded: December 2003
Location: 201 Brotherton Lane, Ferguson
School Architecture: Contemporary, two-story, brick building with some classical features
School Namesake: Named for Berkeley High School, the McCluer School District, and the location within the school district
School History: McCluer South-Berkeley High School was completed in December 2003. Students from Berkeley moved to the new facility in January 2004. (The Grand Opening ceremony was held January 6, 2004.) The cost of the new school will be paid at the expense of the Lambert Airport expansion.
Grades: 9-12
Mascot: "Bulldog"
School Colors: blue and white
School Paper: "Berkeley Newsletter"
School Yearbook: "McCluer South Berkeley High School Bulldog"
Phone Number: 314-506-9800
Website: http://www.fergflor.k12.mo.us/BHS.index.html

McKinley High School

Date Founded: 1904
Location: 3156 Russell between Missouri and Ann Avenues
Land Cost: $26,500 in 1901
Architect: William B. Ittner
School Architecture: All-brick, three-story building that featured twin towers and had the appearance of an 18th-century English castle
Building Cost: $285,957. The electric wiring, heating, plumbing and furnishings were extra.
School Namesake: William McKinley (1843-1901), the 25th President of the U. S.
Site History: The site for the school, on Russell from Missouri to St. Ann Avenue, was purchased in December 1901
School History: McKinley High School was the first St. Louis public high school with manual training

classes. McKinley High School continued until 1925, when it became McKinley Intermediate School. It continued as McKinley Intermediate School until 1932. It then became McKinley High School until 1988. From 1981, the Mass Media Program was held in the building until 1989. In 1989, the Mass Media Program students were transferred to the Central Visual and Performing Arts School (former Yeatman High School) at 3616 N. Garrison Avenue. The original school building is still open; it is currently in use as magnet middle school called "McKinley Classical Junior Academy."
Grades: 9-12
Mascot: "Goldbug." The school's athletic team name was chosen to commemorate the 1896 Republican National Convention, where McKinley supporters wore black pants and gold velvet coats in a parade to signify McKinley's "gold standard" platform.
School Colors: Crimson and white were the initial school colors; later, black and gold
School Flower: Carnation, chosen in honor of the favorite flower of William McKinley
School Paper: Originally called the "Crimson" and, later, the "Goldbug"
School Yearbook: "The Carnation"
Distinguished Awards: Blue Ribbon School by the U. S. Department of Education, 2004
Alumni: Jo Jo White, basketball player

Meda P. Washington High School Program

Date Founded: 1995
Location: 2030 South Vandeventer, St . Louis
Architect: R. M. Milligan
School Namesake: Meda P. Washington, the first presiding judge (1804) of the Court of Quarter Sessions, Louisiana Territory, District of St. Louis.
Site History: Wade Elementary School
School History: The Continued Education High School Program opened in 1969 for continued education of expectant mothers. The program began in the Dumas School at 1409 N. 15th Street and then moved to various locations until 1995, when the name of the program was changed to "Meda P. Washington School." Meda P. Washington opened in 1995 in the Wade Elementary School building at 2030 S. Vandeventer, and the program is still operating at that location.
Grades: 6-12
Current Enrollment: approximately 120 students
Phone Number: 314-771-4067
Website: http://www.slps.mo.us/Schools/high/medap/medap.htm

Mehlville High School (1st location)

Date Founded: 1925
Location: St. John Elementary School, Mehlville
School Architecture: two-story, rectangular, brick building
School Namesake: Charles Mehl, who owned a farm on Lemay Ferry Road
School History: Mehlville High School traces its beginning to 1925, when a ninth grade was added to St. John School. The first high school graduates received their diplomas in 1930. The first separate high school building was dedicated in 1939, with 274 boys and 241 girls attending. In 1955, a new facility became Mehlville, and the original high school became a junior high school. At the present time, the circa-1939 Mehlville High School is used as the Witzel Learning Center.
Grades: 9-12

Mehlville Senior High School

Date Founded: 1925
Location: 3200 Lemay Ferry Road in Mehlville
School Architecture: two-story, rectangular, brick and glass building
School Namesake: Charles Mehl, who owned a farm on Lemay Ferry Road
School History: Mehlville Senior High School is in the Mehville School District and traces its beginning to 1925, when a ninth grade was added to St. John School. The first high school graduates received their diplomas in 1930. The first separate high school building was dedicated in

1939, with 274 boys and 241 girls attending. In 1955, a new facility became Mehlville High School and the original High School became a Junior High School. Presently, the circa-1939 Mehlville High School is used as the Witzel Learning Center. In 2003, the current Mehlville Senior High School went through a major expansion to increase the size of the facility.
Grades: 9-12
Current Enrollment: approximately 2,021 students
Mascot: "Panther"
School Colors: green and white with black
School Paper: "Student Prince"
School Yearbook: "Reflector"
Phone Number: 314-467-6000
Website: http://www.mehlvilleschooldistrict.com

Melvin Ray Eskridge High School

Date Founded: 1962
Location: 1200 Sutter Street in Wellston
School Architect: Hercules Construction
School Architecture: three-story, all-brick high school
School Namesake: Haulter High School, named in honor of Superintendent of Schools, Milliard Haulter; later renamed "Melvin Ray Eskridge High School" in honor of a student.
School History: Wellston High School students transferred to Milliard Haulter High School, named in honor of the Superintendent of Schools, in 1962. In 1978, a student by the name of Melvin Ray Eskridge, who had been diagnosed with terminal cancer, entered the school and began attending classes. Despite his illness, he continued attending school, and his positive attitude made him a role model for the students and the community. He died in 1978 at the age of 14. He had made such an impact on the community that the Board of Education voted to rename the school. In 1979, Haulter High School became Melvin Ray Eskridge High School in his honor.
Grades: 9-12
Current Enrollment: approximately 123 students
Mascot: "Fighting Trojans"
School Colors: red and black
School Paper: "Flashight"
School Yearbook: "WELLHISCO"
Phone Number: 314-290-7800
Website: http://wellston.k12.mo.us/eskridge/index.htp
Alumni: Melvin Ray Eskridge, dedicated student, role model, and namesake for his high school

Metro Academic and Classical High School Program

Date Founded: 1972
Location: 2135 Chouteau in St Louis City
School History: The Metro Academic and Classical High School Program began at 2135 Chouteau until 1980, when it opened at its new location at 5017 Washington. The program continued at the Washington Avenue location until 1997, when it moved to its present location at 4015 McPherson.
Grades: 9-12

Metro Academic and Classical High School (magnet high school)

Date Founded: 1972 at first location, 2135 Chouteau (1972- 1980)
Location: 4015 Mcpherson in St Louis City
School Architecture: modern, segmented, two-story building with an exterior of light-colored stone and glass windows
School Namesake: St. Louis metropolitan area
Site History: Old Marquette Elementary School site
School History: The Metro Academic and Classical High School (magnet high school) program continued at the Washington Avenue location from 1980 to 1997. It became a magnet high school in 1997 when it moved to its present location at 4015 McPherson.
Grades: 9-12
Current Enrollment: approximately 236 students
Mascot: "Panther"
School Colors: gold, black and white
School Paper: "Metro Spirit"
School Yearbook: "Metro Vision"
Distinguished Awards: Blue Ribbon School by the U. S. Department of Education, 2004
Phone Number: 314-534-3894
Website: http://www.slps.k12.mo.us/Schools/high/metro/welcome.htm

Missouri School for the Blind

Date Founded: 1851
Location: 3815 Magnolia, St. Louis City
School Namesake: location and task
School History: The Missouri School for the Blind opened in 1851, and the state of Missouri took over responsibility for the school in 1855. In 1860, it was the first school in the U. S. to adopt the Braille system, which was a revolutionary way for the visually impaired to read.
Current Enrollment: approximately 120 students
Phone Number: (314) 776-4320
Website: webmaster@msb.k12.mo.us

Normal School

Date Founded: 1857
Location: Seventh and Chestnut Streets
School Namesake: a "Normal School" is a facility that trains teachers, chiefly elementary grades; the designation is derived from the French *école normale*, the name of a school founded as a model for other teacher-training schools
School History: Normal School opened in 1857 and was a branch of the first high school. It was located in the 4th story of the Polytechnic Building. The purpose of Normal School was to prepare elementary school teachers for the St. Louis School System. The school required a minimum of two years of study to graduate, and it had a preparatory class that identified the best potential students. In 1875, 220 high school graduates were attending the school.
Grades: 9-12+

Normandy Senior High School

Date Founded: 1923
Location: 6701 St. Charles Rock Road (Easton) in Wellston
School Architecture: multiple four-story, gothic, all-brick buildings laid out in campus style
School Namesake: named for the Normandy School District
Site History: The original site was once Eden Seminary.
School History: Normandy High School began in 1923, when the Normandy School Board purchased Eden Seminary; the facility was used jointly by the seminary and high school for the 1923-1924 school year. The present high school was built on the same property and formally opened on Saturday, October 15, 1925. A fire on August 14, 1949, destroyed the top three floors of the original seminary building. The seminary foundation was totally razed in 1958. The original clock from the Eden Seminary building was preserved and restored, to be used for Centennial reunions in the Administration Building. Normandy Senior High School is located at 6701 St. Charles Rock Road (Easton), in the Normandy School District. The high school still has a "campus" setting, with a quadrangle surrounded by the various halls and buildings.
Grades: 9-12
Current Enrollment: approximately 1,250 students
Mascot: "Vikings." Students named the mascot after the "Vikings" that conquered Normandy, France.
School Colors: red and green
School Paper: originally the "Courier"
School Yearbook: "Saga"
Phone Number: 314-493-0600
Website: http://normandy.k12.mo.us/nhs/aboutnhs.html
Alumni: Ted Drewes (1946) and Dorothy Whemeyer Drewes, co-founders of the popular St. Louis frozen custard stands that bear his name

Normandy Technical High School

Date Founded: 1980
Location: 4333 Goodfellow Boulevard in St. Louis County
School Architecture: the two-story, 4800-square-foot center is designed like a college campus
School Namesake: named for the Normandy School District
Site History: former U. S. Army facility
School History: The St. Louis Job Corps Center is one of 118 Job Corps centers across the country managed by the U. S. Department of Labor. The Job Corps Centers are operated by MINACT, Inc., which provides vocational and academic training. The St. Louis Job Corps Center is affiliated with the Normandy School District, and graduates between the ages of 16 and 20 years of age receive a degree from Normandy Technical High School. Graduates between the ages of 21 and 24 years receive a Graduate Equivalent Degree (GED). The Center currently has 280 male and 168 female students who live in on-campus dormitories and 29 male and 128 female students who commute.
Grades: ages 16-20 years, diploma; 21-24 years, G.E.D.
Current Enrollment: approximately 600 students
Mascot: "Trojans"
School Colors: burgundy and gold
School Paper: "Job Corps Newsletter"
School Yearbook: none
Phone Number: 314-679-6274 (St. Louis Job Corps Center 314-679-0300)
Website: http://stlouisjobcorps.com

North County Technical High School

Date Founded: 1968
Location: 1700 Derhake in Florissant
School Architecture: single-story, contemporary, brick building
School Namesake: location in St. Louis County
School History: North County Technical High School is one of the technical schools operated by St. Louis County Special School District.
Grades: 10-12
Current Enrollment: approximately 1,000 students
Mascot: "Eagle"
School Colors: blue and gold
School Yearbook: "North Tech"
Phone Number: 314-989-7600
Website: http://www.ssd.k12.mo.us/Tech_ed/Schools/North_Tech/n_tech.html

Northview High School

Date Founded: 1964
Location: 1520 Derhake, St. Louis County
Architect: Kenneth Wischmeyer
School Architecture: Contemporary ranch style
School Namesake: location in St. Louis County
School History: Northview is a Special School District facility for students with severe handicaps.
Grades: 9-12
Current Enrollment: approximately 180 students
Mascot: "Northview Eagle"
School Colors: black and gold
School Paper: None
School Yearbook: Occasionally
Phone Number: 314-989-7300

Northwest High School

Date Founded: 1950s
Location: 6005 Cedar Hill Road, Jefferson County
School Architecture: Contemporary
School Namesake: location and school district
School History: Northwest High School is located in Northwest R-1 school district in Jefferson County.
Grades: 9-12
Current Enrollment: approximately 2,200 students
Mascot: "Lions"
School Colors: blue and white
School Paper: "The Detail"
School Yearbook: "Lion Trac"
Phone Number: 636-274-0555
Website: http://www.nwhsr1.com

Northwest High School

Date Founded: 1964
Location: 5140 Riverview, St. Louis City
Architect: Charles Huning
School Architecture: three-story, contemporary, brick building
Building Cost: $3,600,000
School Namesake: location in northwest part of St. Louis City
School History: Northwest High School opened in 1964. It was built to relieve the overcrowding at Beaumont High School. Northwest was constructed on a six-acre site in the 5100 block of Riverview Boulevard, adjoining Davis Park in the Walnut Park neighborhood. The school had a capacity for about 1,200 students but lacked a swimming pool and sufficient gymnasium and auditorium space. A 12-room addition was built in 1968 to increase its capacity to 1,600. The high school closed in 1993 and was re-opened as a middle school.
Grades: 9-12

Oakville Senior High School

Date Founded: 1974
Location: 5557 Milburn Road in St. Louis County
School Architecture: three-story, contemporary, brick building
School Namesake: named after local community
School History: Oakville Senior High School is located in the Mehlville School District.
Grades: 9-12
Current Enrollment: approximately 2,021 students
Mascot: "Tigers"
School Colors: black and gold
School Paper: "Prowl"
School Yearbook: "Tiger Paws"
Phone Number: 314-467-7000
Website: http://www.mehlvilleschooldistrict.com

Opportunity Alternative High School Program

Date Founded: 1966
Location: 5017 Washington Avenue in St. Louis City
School History: In 1967, the school was named "Lincoln High School Opportunity Program."
Grades: 9-12

Parkway Junior-Senior High School

Date Founded: 1957
Location: 471 N. Woods Mill Road in Chesterfield
Architect: Hellmuth Obata and Kassabaum (HOK)
School Architecture: single-story, contemporary, brick and glass building
School Namesake: Daniel Boone Parkway and Parkway School District
Site History: In 1957, Parkway Junior-Senior High School (now Central Middle School) was constructed on 125 acres at the corner of Woods Mill and Ladue Roads. Central High School was founded in 1958 as a coeducational high school. It was named "Parkway Junior-Senior High School" in what is now Parkway Central Middle School, at 471 N. Woods Mill Road in Chesterfield. Later, when new facilities were built, it became "Parkway Central High School," located at 369 N. Woods Mill Road.
Grades: 7-12

Parkway High School

Date Founded: 1961
Location: 369 N. Woods Mill Road in Chesterfield
Architect: Hellmuth Obata and Kassabaum (HOK)
School Architecture: single-story, contemporary, brick and glass building
School Namesake: Daniel Boone Parkway, Parkway School District and location
School History: In 1961, Parkway High School (now Parkway Central Senior High School) was completed, and ninth- through 12th-grade students from Parkway Junior-Senior High School transferred to the new high school.
Grades: 9-12
Current Enrollment: approximately 1,400 students
Mascot: "Colt"
School Colors: black, red and white
School Paper: "Corral"
School Yearbook: "Spur"

Parkway Central High School

Date Founded: 1968
Location: 369 N. Woods Mill Road in Chesterfield
Architect: Hellmuth Obata and Kassabaum (HOK)
School Architecture: single-story, contemporary, brick and glass building
School Namesake: Daniel Boone Parkway, Parkway School District and location
School History: In 1968, when Parkway West High School opened as the second high school in the district, Parkway High School's name was changed to "Parkway Central High School." During its short history, Parkway housed the "West" students in 1967; the first "North" students; and finally, from 1974-1976, "South" students.
Grades: 9-12
Current Enrollment: approximately 1,400 students
Mascot: "Colt"
School Colors: black, red and white
School Paper: "Corral"
School Yearbook: "Spur"
Distinguished Awards: Blue Ribbon School by the U. S. Department of Education, 1987, and Missouri Gold Star School, 1987
Phone Number: 314-415-7500
Website: http://www.pkwy.k12.mo.us/centralh/centralh/index.htm

Parkway North High School

Date Founded: 1971
Location: 12860 Fee Fee Road in Creve Coeur
Architect: Hoffman/Saur & Associates
School Architecture: Contemporary, brick and glass, two-story, open school with a variety of building forms
School Namesake: Daniel Boone Parkway, Parkway School District and location
School History: Parkway North High School was founded as a coeducational public high school in the Parkway School District. In 1971, the students attended double sessions at "Central" while the new high school was built. Students moved into the new building in August 1972. Parkway "North" was the first Parkway High School to have its own swimming pool. The educational space is made flexible for changing needs by 30-foot spans on the first level and 60-foot spans above the first level.
Grades: 9-12
Current Enrollment: approximately 1,378 students
Mascot: "Vikings"

School Colors: purple, red and white
School Slogan: "Purple Pride"
School Paper: "Norsestar"
School Yearbook: "Saga"
Distinguished Awards: Blue Ribbon School by the U. S. Department of Education, 1985, and Missouri Gold Star School, 1985
Phone Number: 314-415-7600
Website: http://www.pkwy.k12.mo.us/north

Parkway South High School

Date Founded: 1976
Location: 801 Hanna Road in Manchester
School Architecture: two-story, contemporary, brick and glass building
School Namesake: Daniel Boone Parkway, Parkway School District and location
School History: Parkway South High School started in the bicentennial year of 1976 as a public, coeducational high school in the Parkway School District.
Grades: 9-12
Current Enrollment: approximately 2,168 students
Mascot: "Patriots"
School Colors: red, white and Navy blue
School Hallmark: "Patriot Pride"
School Paper: "Treaty"
School Yearbook: "The Declaration"
Distinguished Awards: Blue Ribbon School by the U. S. Department of Education, 1987, 1996 and Missouri Gold Star School, 1987, 1996
Phone Number: 314-415-7700
Website: http://pshwired.net/unleashed/index.php

Parkway West High School

Date Founded: 1968
Location: 14653 Clayton Road in Ballwin
School Architecture: two-story, brick and glass, contemporary building
School Namesake: Daniel Boone Parkway, Parkway School District and location
School History: Parkway West High School began in 1968 as a coeducational, public high school in the Parkway School District.

Grades: 9-12
Current Enrollment: approximately 1,543 students
Mascot: the "Longhorns"
School Colors: Columbian blue, red and white
School Motto: "West is Best"
School Paper: "Pathfinder"
School Yearbook: "PAWESEHI"
Distinguished Awards: Blue Ribbon School by the U. S. Department of Education, 1983, and Missouri Gold Star School, 1983
Phone Number: 314-415-7500
Website: http://www.pkwy.k12.mo.us/west/westsr.html
Alumni: Stone Phillips, NBC-TV news personality; and August Busch IV, St. Louis brewery executive

Pattonville High School

Date Founded: 1935
Location: Banks and St. Charles Rock Roads in St. Louis County
Land Cost: $6,400
Architect: William B. Ittner
School Namesake: Patton family that owned a store on the corner of Fee Fee Road and St. Charles Rock Road, and the Pattonville School District.
School History: Pattonville High School opened in 1935 and was located on eight acres at Banks and St. Charles Rock Roads in the Pattonville School District. The land was purchased for $800 per acre. The first graduation class, in 1937, consisted of two students. The high school closed in 1971, when the new high school opened on Creve Coeur Mill Road. The site of the original building is now the Pattonville Learning Center.
Grades: 9-12

Pattonville Senior High School

Date Founded: 1971
Location: 2497 Creve Coeur Mill Road in Maryland Heights
Architect: Gale A. Hill and Associates designed the auditorium, and Parsons Brickerhoff designed the new library and science center.
School Architecture: The building is masonry with steel framing, concrete floors, bar joists and EDPM roofing.
Building Cost: $4,500,000 for auditorium; $2,300,000 for library; $4,500,000 for science wing
School Namesake: Patton family, which owned a store on the corner of Fee Fee Road and St. Charles Rock Road; Pattonville School District.
School History: Pattonville Senior High School opened in 1971 in the building that was a 7th-grade center, located at 2497 Creve Coeur Mill Road in Maryland Heights, in the Pattonville School District. The school served grades 10-12 until 1981, when it began serving grades 9-12.
Grades: 9-12
Current Enrollment: 950 female and 997 male students
Mascot: "Pirate"
School Colors: green and white
School Paper: "Pirate Press"
School Yearbook: "Echo"
Phone Number: 314-213-8051
Website: http://www.psdr3.org
Alumni: Kent Ehrhardt, chief meteorologist on KMOV-TV: John Hancock, state legislator; Heather Smith, "Miss Missouri 1987;" Brent Roam, actor; and Janet Jones, actress (and wife of hockey great Wayne Gretzky)

Pruitt Alternative High School

Date Founded: 1976
Location: 1212 N. 22nd Street
School History: The Pruitt Alternative High School Program opened in 1976 at 1212 N. 22nd; the program continued until 1982.
Grades: 9-12

Public Safety and Junior NROTC High School Program

Date Founded: 1981
Location: 5031 Potomac in St. Louis City
School Namesake: U. S. Navy

Site History: the Kennard Elementary School building
School History: Public Safety and Junior NROTC (Junior Naval Reserved Officer Training Corps) opened in 1981 in the Kennard School building. The program continued at that location until 1984, when it was moved to Cleveland High School at 4352 Louisiana.
Grades: 9-12

Public School Library

Date Founded: 1865
Location: Fifth and Olive Streets
History: Public School Library opened in 1865 in the Derby Building; in 1869, it moved to Fifth and Olive.
Grades: 9-12

Ritenour High School

Date Founded: 1911
Location: 8740 Forest Avenue (now 2500 Marshall Avenue) in St. Louis County
School Namesake: J. S. Ritenour, a prominent landowner who died on March 29, 1867
School History: Ritenour High School began in 1911, when the first students attended high school classes in a grade school. The first public, coeducational high school building was built in 1924 and was located in the Ritenour Senior School District.
Grades: 9-12

Ritenour Senior High School

Date Founded: 1950
Location: 9100 St. Charles Rock Road in Overland
Land Cost: $10 first parcel
Architect: William B. Ittner, Inc.
School Architecture: three-story, brick and glass, Art Deco-style building
Building Cost: $1,927,180 original building
School Namesake: J. S. Ritenour, a prominent landowner who died on March 29, 1867
School History: Ritenour Senior High School opened 1950 as a coeducational, public high school in the Ritenour School District.
Current Enrollment: 892 female and 866 male students
Mascot: "Husky" (dog)
School Colors: black and orange
School Paper: "Pepper Box"
School Yearbook: "Melareus"
Phone Number: 314-493-6105
Website: http://www.ritenour.k12.mo.us

Riverview Gardens High School (1st location)

Date Founded: 1927
Location: 805 Chambers Road
School History: Riverview Gardens Senior High School
Riverview Gardens Senior High School opened in 1927 in the old Science Hill School, built in 1926. It was located at 805 Chambers Road until a new facility was built in 1950. The building then became East Junior High School.
Grades: 9-12

Riverview Gardens High School (2nd location)

Date Founded: 1957
Location: 8024 Benton Avenue in St. Louis County

School Architecture: campus-style, single-story, light-colored brick building
School Namesake: named for Riverview Gardens School District
Site History: Farmland
School History: Riverview Gardens Senior High School opened in 1950 as a public, coeducational high school in the Riverview Gardens School District.
Grades: 9-12
Current Enrollment: approximately 1,900 students
Mascot: "Ram"
School Colors: Royal blue and gold
School Paper: "The View"
School Yearbook: "Echoes"
Phone Number: 314-869-4700
Website: http://www.rgsd.org/html/highschool.html
Alumni: Bob Kuban, St. Louis bandleader

Rock Spring Alternative High School

Date Founded: 1976
Location: 3974 Sarpy in St. Louis City
Architect: William B. Ittner
School Architecture: four-story, rectangular, brick building
School Namesake: named for location
Site History: Rock Spring Elementary School
School History: The Rock Spring Alternative High School Program began in 1976 in the Rock Spring Elementary School building at 3974 Sarpy. The program continued at that location until 1980. Erected in 1899, the building is vacant but still standing.
Grades: 9-12

Rockwood Summit Senior High School

Date Founded: 1994
Location: 1780 Hawkins Road in Fenton
School Architecture: two-story, brick and glass, contemporary building
School Namesake: School District
Site History: Rockwood Summit Senior High School is located in the Rockwood School District.
Grades: 9 -12
Current Enrollment: approximately 1,382 students.
Mascot: "Falcon"
School Colors: maroon, black and silver
School Paper: "Talon"
School Yearbook: "Pinnacle"
Phone Number: 636-861-7700
Website:http://www.rockwood.k12.mo.us/rsummit/

Roosevelt High School

Date Founded: opened January 26, 1925
Location: 3240 Hartford
Architect: Rockwell M. Milligan
School Architecture: brick, English Renaissance, three-story building
Building Cost: $1,498,109
School Namesake: Theodore Roosevelt (1858-1919), 26th President of the United States (1901-1905 and 1905-1909)

Site History: The school was built on the site of Holy Ghost (the old Picker) Cemetery. Evacuation of the cemetery began October 16, 1922, and the cornerstone for the school was laid April 22, 1923.
School History: Roosevelt High School opened January 26, 1925, as a public high school. The school was built under the name of "New Southside High School" but was renamed to honor of Theodore Roosevelt. The school song carries the melody of Harvard's school song (Harvard was Roosevelt's *alma mater*).
Grades: 9-12
Current Enrollment: 1,896 students
Mascot: "Teddy Bear" and "Rough Riders"
School Colors: crimson and white (colors are the same as Harvard University's)
School Paper: "The Rough Rider"
School Yearbook: "Bwana"
Phone Number: 314-776-6040
Website: http://www.acumen-corp.com/rhs

St. Charles High School

Date Founded: 1924 (founded in 1901)
Location: 725 North Kingshighway Street in St. Charles City
Building Cost: $155,217 for the 1922 high school
School Namesake: St. Charles City
Site History: built on the site of St. Charles Military College
School History: St. Charles High School began in 1901 as a two-year, public, coeducational high school in Jefferson School at Fourth and Jefferson Streets. In 1918, a fire partially destroyed the building, and the high school moved into the vacant St. Charles Military College. It remained there until 1923, when a bond issue financed the construction of a new facility at the same location. The present St. Charles High School opened at that location in 1924 and has grown through the years. As the population increased, so did the school. Moreover, new school districts were incorporated, including Fort Zumwalt School District in 1949, Orchard Farm School District in 1959, Francis Howell and Wentzville.
Grades: 9-12
Enrollment: approximately 1,100 students
Mascot: "Fighting Pirates"
School Song: "How We Love You St. Charles High School"
School Colors: Navy blue and white
School Paper: "Pirate Patter and Ship's Log"
School Yearbook: "Charlemo"
Phone Number: 636-724-3940
Website: http://www.stcharles.k12.mo.us/schigh/admin.htm
Alumni: KSDK-TV news anchor Art Holliday

St. Charles West High School

Date Founded: 1976
Location: 3601 Droste Road in St. Charles City
School Namesake: St. Charles City
School History: St. Charles West High School opened in 1976 as a public, coeducational high school.
Grades: 9-12
Enrollment: approximately 1,030 students
Mascot: "Warriors"
School Colors: maroon and white
School Paper: "The Smoke Signal"
School Yearbook: "Trailblazer"
Phone Number: 636-723-7900
Website: http://www.stcharles.k12.mo.us/scwest

St. Louis Colored Orphans Home

Date Founded: 1888
Location: 1427 North 12th Street
School History: St. Louis Colored Orphans Home was founded 1888 by Mrs. Sarah Newton. A new building for the home was erected in 1922 at 2612 Goode Avenue with gift money and land from Annie Malone. In 1946, the home was renamed in her honor.

Senior Classical Academy High School Program

Date Founded: 1981
Location: 918 N. Union in St. Louis City
Site History: Soldan High School
The Senior Classical Academy High School Program began in 1981 in Soldan High School, at 918 N. Union. The program remained there until 1990, when it moved into Roosevelt High School, at 3230 Hartford Road; it ended in 1992.
Grades: 9-12

Soldan High School

Date Founded: September 1909
Location: 918 N. Union Boulevard
Land Cost: $10,000
Architect: William B. Ittner
School Architecture: Gothic Tudor Revival-style of 1620; three-story, all-brick building with 77 classrooms
Building Cost: $630,244
School Namesake: Frank Louis Soldan (1842-1908), who had been Assistant Superintendent of Schools (1870-1872). He was also Normal School principal (1872-1887), High and Normal School principal (1887-1895), and Superintendent of Schools (1895-1908).
Site History: The site purchased for the school was 306 feet by 390 feet.
School History: Soldan High School opened in September 1909. The school was built to be "New High School" but was opened under the name of "Soldan High School" in honor of Frank Louis Soldan. The size of the school is 288 feet by 256 feet. In 1948, the school was renamed "Soldan-Blewett High School" when Soldan High and Blewett High (previously located at 5321 Enright) combined and shared the building. Blewett High School is one block east of Soldan on Enright. Because the building was overcrowded, portable buildings were erected at 5323 Cates Avenue. The new building opened in September 1962. In 1955, the name of the school changed from "Soldan-Blewett" back to "Soldan High School" until 1990. In 1993, the school reopened as a magnet school and is now called the "Soldan International Studies High School."
Grades: 9-12
Mascot: Soldan "Wildcats"
School Paper: "The Scrip"
Phone Number: 314-367-9222
Website: http://www.ics.addr.com/soldan.html
Alumni: William McChesney Martin Jr., first paid New York Stock Exchange president (1938) and chairman of the Federal Reserve Board (1951-1970); Tennessee Williams, attendee, famous American playwright; A. E. Hotchner, author and (with actor Paul Newman) salad dressing mogul; Virginia Mayo, actress; Kay Thompson, singer, songwriter, author; Clark Clifford, Washington attorney and advisor to several U. S. presidents; Agnes Moorehead, actress.

Soldan-Blewett High School

Date Founded: 1948
Location: 918 N. Union Boulevard
Land Cost: $10,000

Architect: William B. Ittner
School Architecture: Gothic Tudor Revival-style of 1620; three-story, all-brick building with 77 classrooms
Building Cost: $630,244
School Namesake: Frank Louis Soldan and Ben Blewett
Site History: Soldan High School
School History: Renamed Soldan High School in 1955 (*see above*).
Grades: 9-12

Soldan International High School Studies Program (magnet high school)

Date Founded: 1993
Location: 918 N. Union
Land Cost: $10,000
Architect: William B. Ittner
School Architecture: Gothic Tudor Revival-style of 1620; three-story, all-brick building with 77 classrooms
Building Cost: $630,244
School Namesake: Frank Louis Soldan (1842-1908)
Site History: Soldan International Studies (Magnet High School)
The Soldan International High School Studies Program opened in 1993 as an International Studies magnet in the Soldan High School Building at 918 N. Union. The school is located just north of Forest Park in the western end of St. Louis's historic Union-Delmar neighborhood. All St. Louis-area middle schools serve as feeder schools for Soldan International Studies High School. The Bunche International Studies Middle School, with its identical magnet theme, serves as a direct sequential feeder. The magnet focus is world languages and world culture, which enables students to develop skills in problem solving, technology and language proficiency.
Grades: 9-12
Current Enrollment: approximately 840 students
Mascot: "Tiger"
School Colors: maroon and gold
School Paper: "Scripts;" now "Soldan World"
School Yearbook: "World Vision;" now "Soldan"
Phone Number: 314-367-9222

South County Technical High School

Date Founded: 1967
Location: 12721 West Watson in Sunset Hills
Architect: Kenneth E. Wischmeyer and Partners
School Architecture: single-story, brick and glass, campus style
School Namesake: south part of St. Louis County
School History: South County Technical High School is one of the technical schools operated by St. Louis County Special School District.
Grades: 10-12
Current Enrollment: approximately 1,000
Mascot: "Hawks"
School Colors: red, white and black
School Paper: none
School Yearbook: "Memories"
Phone Number: 314-989-7400
Website: http://www.ssd.k12.mo.us/Tech_ed/Schools/South_Tech/s_tech.htm
Alumni: "Towel Man" at Blues Hockey games; Murphy Lee, who plays in rapper Nelly's band

South Grand Work-Study High School Program

Date Founded: 1969
Location: 1530 South Grand Avenue in St. Louis City
School Namesake: Location, Grand Avenue
School History: The work-study program continued at that location until 1979.
Grades: 9-12

Southview School

Date Founded: 1979
Location: 11660 Eddie and Park Road in Crestwood
School History: Southview School is one of five special education schools operated by Special School District of St. Louis County. The school educates students with a range of disabilities from ages 5 to 21 years. The school has two major program areas for students: one for students with developmental disabilities, the other for students with behavioral disorders.
Current Enrollment: approximately 171 students
Mascot: "Cougar"
School Colors: red and white
School Paper: None
School Yearbook: "Memories"
Phone Number: 314-989-8900
Website: http://www.ssd.k12.mo.us/Sp_edu/Schools/southview/index.html

Southwest High School

Date Founded: September 7, 1937
Location: 3125 South Kingshighway, in the Southwest neighborhood
Land Cost: $67,414
Architect: George W. Sanger
School Architecture: three-story, square-shaped facility with a fourth floor in the center made of red sandstone colonial brick. Except for the five large symbolic figures overlooking the main doors dominating the entrance, the school is plain in comparison with earlier St. Louis high schools. In 1964, the three-sided section was built on Kingshighway, enclosing the outer court. The athletic field

Photo courtesy of St. Louis Public Schools Records Center/Archives.

was removed from the front of the building to accommodate the addition designed by Kenneth Wischmeyer (outside architect). The athletic field is now in the rear of the school.
Building Cost: $676,921. The cost of the first addition was $432,906, and the second, $1,803,005
School Namesake: location, the southwest part of St. Louis City
Site History: The location had been part of Kemper College, an Episcopalian institution that opened in 1838 and closed in 1845 because of financial problems; some of its buildings were used by the County Poor House. Near the turn of the century, Koerner's Summer Garden occupied the site.
School History: Southwest High School was built as a WPA project and opened September 7, 1937, as a public high school. The cost of the property was $67,414, and the cost to build the school was $676,921. Fred Morie of St. Louis sculpted the figures. As a group they represent "Youthful Leadership," but individually they have been interpreted as "Exact Sciences," "Social Interests," Youthful Leadership," "The Liberal Arts," and "Athletic Activities." School legend has it that the statues were added in place of a swimming pool. Southwest High School was the first 20th-century St. Louis City public high school to be named for a geographic area rather than for a famous person. In 1957, to accommodate increased enrollment, an addition was made on its northern side. Now, one can see the five magnificent statues only by looking through the entrance gate on Arsenal. Southwest High School closed at the end of the 1992-1993 school year. The Records Center/ Archives briefly occupied the facility. In 1994, during the renovation of Roosevelt High School, the building served as "Roosevelt at Southwest" to the end of 1995 school year. It also has been used

by Mathews-Dickey Boys' Club and Community Access Job Training (CAJT) and by the Career Education Academy. In July 2004, the St Louis School District announced that Central Visual and Performing Arts High School was closing and the students would transfer and begin the fall 2004 school year in the building that once was the home of Southwest High School.
Grades: 9-12
Mascot: "Longhorns," "SNAFU"
School Colors: green and gold
School Motto: "Enter to learn; go forth to serve."
School Paper: "Pioneer"
School Yearbook: "Roundup"
Alumni: Richard Gephardt, U.S. Congressman

Sumner High School (1st location)

Date Founded: March 1875
Location: 11th and Spruce Streets
Land Cost: $22,500
School Architecture: A contemporary, three-story, rectangular, all-brick building with no outstanding ornamentation other than an arch over the doors and a small column on either side of them. It had 12 rooms with seating for 700 students.
Building Cost: $28,500
School Namesake: The school was named in honor of Charles Sumner (1811-1874), American statesman, abolitionist, and U. S. senator from Massachusetts.
Site History: Washington Elementary School from 1860-1875
School History: Charles Sumner High School began in March 1875 by an Act of the Missouri General Assembly "for the purpose of educating the colored children of the City of St. Louis in advanced studies." In 1890, the school established a Normal Department for the purpose of giving Sumner High School graduates special preparation for the work of teaching, and thus placing the schools for "colored" children on an equal standing with the schools for white children with regard to qualification of teachers. The June 1886 School Board records reported, "That when opportunity offers, the building and lot occupied by the Sumner High School be disposed of at a favorable opportunity, it being objectionable for school purposes on account of the nearness of the railroad, and the unhealthy situation, and that a higher and more salubrious site be purchased for the school." After the committee visited the school they reported, "The only objection that can be urged to the school is the proximity of the Union Depot, the Four Courts and the Morgue." The Class of 1895 had 27 graduates. In 1897, the high school was moved to a new location at 15th and Walnut Streets in St. Louis City.
Grades: 9-12
Enrollment: 210 students in 1894-1895

Sumner High School (2nd location)

Date Founded: 1897
Location: 15th and Walnut Streets
School Architecture: three-story, rectangular, brick building
School Namesake: Charles Sumner (1811-1874), American statesman, abolitionist, and U. S. Senator from Massachusetts.
Site History: Eliot Elementary School from 1868–1897
School History: In 1897, the School Board records

reported the following: "At the beginning of the year just closed, Sumner High School was happily removed from the old and dilapidated building at Eleventh and Spruce Streets, a site which it had occupied for many years, the new, and much superior location at Fifteenth and Walnut Streets." The second Sumner High School location (which was in the second Eliot Grammar School building) was at 15th and Walnut until 1910.
Grades: 9-12

Sumner High School (3rd location) (magnet school)

Date Founded: September 1910
Location: 4248 W. Cottage Avenue in the "Ville" Neighborhood
Land Cost: $15, 940
Architect: William B. Ittner
School Architecture: Georgian Revival, three-story, all-brick building
Building Cost: $311,665
School Namesake: Charles Sumner (1811-1874), American statesman, abolitionist, and U.S. Senator from Massachusetts
School History: Sumner High School opened in its third and present location in the Ville neighborhood in September 1910. The Ville is bounded by St. Louis Avenue on the north, Martin Luther King Drive on the south, Sarah on the east and Taylor on the north. The initial location of Sumner, St. Louis's first black high school, was at 11th and Spruce Streets (1875-1898); the second location for the high school was at 15th and Walnut (1898-1910). In March 1911, Sumner became the first "colored" (black) school admitted to the North Central Association of High Schools and Colleges.
Grades: 9-12
Current Enrollment: 905 students
Mascot: Sumner "Bulldogs"
School Colors: maroon and white
School Paper: formerly "The Collegiate;" none at present
School Yearbook: "The Maroon and White"
Phone Number: 314-371-1048
Website: http://www.slps.org.Schools/mega/sumner2/INDEX>HTML
Alumni: Dick Gregory; comedian and political activist; Metropolitan opera singers Grace Bumbry and Robert McFerrin; rock 'n roll stars Chuck Berry and Tina Turner; tennis great Arthur Ashe; Julius Hunter, former KMOV-TV news anchor; musician Olesier Lake; General Roscoe Robinson, pilot; Wendell Pruett, war hero; and artist Manuel Hughes

Tri-A Outreach Center I High School Program

Date Founded: 1984
Location: 1909 N. Kingshighway in St. Louis City
Site History: formerly McBride High School and then Martin Luther King, Jr., High School
School History: The Tri-A Outreach Center I High School Program was an alternative education program. "Tri-A" stands for "Attendance, Attitude, and Achievement" and represents the three key steps required to succeed in school. The program was initially located in Mathews-Dickey building and continued there until 1993, when the program was transferred to the former McBride High School (and then Martin Luther King, Jr., High School) building at 1909 North Kingshighway. The program was discontinued in 2003.
Grades: 9-12

Tri-A Outreach Center II High School Program

Date Founded: 1994
Location: 1909 N. Kingshighway in St. Louis City
Site History: formerly McBride High School and then Martin Luther King Jr., High School
School History: The Tri-A Outreach Center II High School Program was an alternative education program, initially located in the Madison Elementary School building at 1118 South Seventh Street. In 2000, enrolled students

transferred to the King Tri-A Outreach Center (formerly McBride High School and then Martin Luther King, Jr., High School building) at 1909 North Kingshighway. The program was discontinued in 2003. In September 2000, the Madison Elementary School building reopened as an elementary school.
Grades: 9-12

Turner Open Air School

Date Founded: 1925
School History: Turner Open Air School was founded by the St. Louis Board of Education in 1925. The school provided services for black children with orthopedic disabilities or hearing impairment, and those at risk for tuberculosis (TB).
Grades: 9-12

University City Senior High School

Date Founded: 1911; 1930 present school
Location: 7401 Balson Avenue in University City
Architect: Trueblood and Graff architects, and Ferrand and Fitch, associated architects, designed the high school. William B. Ittner designed the auditorium, built in 1936; and the recently constructed natatorium was designed by Pearce and Pearce.
School Architecture: Modern for the period. Art Deco details including reed pilasters, and stylized plant forms around the main entrance. The pyramidal roof is set behind a parapet wall with beveled coping.
School Namesake: named for University City
School History: The University City high school began in a flat rented from Mr. Frazier at 6702 Delmar Avenue for $26 per month. The same year, it moved to portable building at 6605-7 Bartmer Avenue (now Pershing Avenue). In 1912, because of an influx of new students, the school moved to the 2nd floor of the Press Room Building. In 1913, it moved to the Delmar School. In 1915, University City acquired the Fine Arts building, which was used as the first high school. Land for the present University City Senior High School was purchased in 1923 and 1924, and the school construction began in 1928.
Grades: 9-12
Current Enrollment: approximately 1,120 students
Mascot: "Indians"
School Colors: black and gold
School Paper: "Tom Tom"
School Yearbook: "Dial"
Phone Number: 314-290-4100
Website: http://www.ucityschools.org/schools/highschool.htm
Alumni: Rap artist Nelly (Cornell Haynes, Jr.); Tennessee Williams, playwright; Eric Mink, *St. Louis Post-Dispatch* newspaper columnist; Dave Garraway, original host of NBC's "Today" show

Valley Park High School

Date Founded: September 6, 1932
Location: One Main Street (formerly 356 Meramec Station Road) in Valley Park
School History: Valley Park High School began on September 6, 1932, as a coeducational, public high school; the first class graduated two years later. It is the nucleus for the present campus for Valley Park High School, located in the Valley Park School District. The original, two-story high school building has remained. In 1989, a new addition was added to the high school; and, in 1999 an 11,000-square-foot, two-story

addition provided a library and computer and science laboratories. Recent rerouting of Highway 141 created a new address for the school.
Grades: 9-12
Current Enrollment: approximately 266 students
Mascot: "Hawk"
School Colors: orange and Royal blue
School Paper: "Valley Breeze"
School Yearbook: "VAL-E-VUES"
Phone Number: 636-923-3613
Website: http://www.vp.k12.mo.us/hschool/index.htm

Vashon High School (1st location)

Date Founded: September 6, 1927
Location: 3026 Laclede Avenue, St. Louis City
Architect: Rockwell M. Milligan
Building Cost: $1,180,790
School Namesake: Vashon was named in honor of George Boyer Vashon, the first black graduate of Oberlin College (1824-1878), and John Boyer Vashon (1859-1924), who were educators.
School History: Vashon High School opened on September 6, 1927, as "Vashon High and Intermediate School." Between 1932 and 1934, the "Colored" Vocational High School was located within Vashon High School. On June 11, 1963, the Vashon students moved from what was called "Vashon High School" at 3026 Laclede to a new location that had previously been Hadley Vocational School, at 3405 Bell. Vashon High School remained at 3405 Bell from 1963 until it closed in 2002. The original Vashon building at 3026 Laclede became Harris Teachers College and exists today as part of Harris Stowe Teachers College.
Grades: 9-12
Mascot: "The Wolverine"
School Colors: blue and white
School Paper: "The Herald"
School Yearbook: "Blue and White"
School Song: "Vashon We Love"
Alumni: Henry Armstrong, world boxing champion; Clark Terry, musician; Federal Judge Theodore McMillan; musician Donny Hathaway; and U. S. Congresswoman Maxine Carr Waters.

Vashon High School (2nd location)

Date Founded: 1963
Location: 3405 Bell Avenue in St. Louis City
School Architecture: looks like a large, industrial manufacturing plant
Site History: November 1931, as "Hadley Vocational/Technical High School"
School History: On June 11, 1963, the Vashon students were transferred to the building that previously had been Hadley Vocational School. In August 2002, it moved to a newly constructed modern school building at 3055 Cass. Hadley Vocational School no longer exists. The Vashon building at 3405 Bell was demolished in August 2002. The new site for the high school is in a new building at 3405 Bell, and it is now called "Clyde C. Miller Career Academy."
Grades: 9-12

Vashon High School (3rd location)

Date Founded: 2003
Location: 3035 Cass
Architect: Kennedy & Associates
School Architecture: Contemporary, light and dark brick with a futuristic main entrance

Building Cost: $47,300,000
School Namesake: Vashon was named in honor of George Boyer Vashon, the first black graduate of Oberlin College (1824-1878), and John Boyer Vashon (1859-1924), who were educators.
School History: Vashon High School reopened in 2003 at its new location at 3035 Cass. The area of the school is 230,000 square feet. The Vashon building at 3405 Bell was demolished in August 2002 and is the site for the new Clyde C. Miller Career Academy.
Grades: 9-12
Current Enrollment: approximately 1,208 students
Mascot: "Wolverine"
School Colors: Royal blue and white
School Motto: "Vashon by Choice, the Right Choice"
School Paper: "The Herald"
School Yearbook: 'Blue and White"
Phone Number: 314-533-9487
Website: http://www.slps.k12.mo.us/Schools/high_2.htm

W. F. Gaunt High School (*see* Affton High School)

Washington High School

Date Founded: 1907
Location: St. Charles Rock Road, Normandy
Architect: constructed by John Oth
School Architecture: single-story, two-room, brick building
School Cost: $3,600
School Namesake: George Washington, first president of the United States
Site History: formerly an elementary school, built in 1895
School History: Prior to 1907, students interested in attending school beyond eighth grade had to attend high school in one of the surrounding district schools, hire a tutor, or attend in another city. In St. Louis, the first students attended high school in 1907, in a vacant room of the recently constructed Lincoln School at 6815 Robbins. Later in the school year, the class moved to the old Washington elementary school building on St. Charles Rock Road. The first and only graduation class, in 1911, had only four members. Lack of money and problems getting accredited caused the school to close in the spring of 1912. The building and property were sold to Frank Maxwell for $6,000. In 1923, it was decided to open another high school because it was costing more than $5,000 a year to send students to other districts. In 1923, Eden Seminary was purchased for $200,000 in bonds and became the first Normandy High School.
Grades: 9-12
Current Enrollment: building could accommodate 100 students

Webster Groves High School (1st location)

Date Founded: 1889
Location: Selma Avenue in Webster Groves
School Architecture: two-story, brick building with three classrooms and an auditorium
School Namesake: named for the city of Webster Groves
School History: Webster Groves High began in 1889, when a high school program was offered for ninth graders. In 1916, the high school occupied the first floor of the original 20 Gray Avenue Building, which was later named "Bristol School." In 1905, the high school classes were moved to the second floor of the Brannon Building on Gore Avenue, north of the Missouri Pacific Railroad tracks. In 1906, the district built a high school on Selma Avenue, a two-story, brick building with three classrooms and an auditorium.
Grades: 9-12

Webster Groves High School (2nd location)

Date Founded: 1924
Location: 100 Selma Avenue in Webster Groves
School Architecture: three-story, red brick building with ornamental stone trim
School Namesake: Frank Hampsher, school superintendent (1917-1924)
School History: Following World War I, the high school moved into the Webster Groves Armory. Constructed in 1917, it was turned over to the high school and housed the lunchroom and senior gymnasium. In 1924, a new high school was built and named after Frank Hampsher, school superintendent from 1917-24, and called the "Frank Hampsher High School." The present Webster Groves High School is a coeducational, public high school in the Webster Groves School District. It has gone through a number of expansions. The well-known football rivalry between Webster Groves High School and Kirkwood High School began in 1907. The winner of their annual Thanksgiving Day game receives the Frisco "Bell," and the loser, the "Little Brown Jug."
Grades: 9-12
Current Enrollment: approximately 1,387 students
Mascot: "Statesmen"
School Colors: orange and black
School Paper: "ECHO"
School Yearbook: "ECHO"
Phone Number: 314-963-6400
Website: http://www.webster.k12.mo.us/wghs
Alumni: Harry Caray, the Chicago baseball announcer

Wellston High School

Date Founded: 1906
Location: 6301 Wells Avenue at Evergreen in Wellston
School Architecture: two-story, all-brick building with 19 classrooms
School Namesake: Named after school district and Erastus Wells, founder of Wellston
School History: Wellston High School was organized in 1906. The high school was located in one room of the Central Building, and the first class graduated in May 1911. Wellston High School opened in 1923 and was located at 6301 Wells Avenue in the Wellston School District. When Milliard Haulter High School opened in 1962, the Wellston students were transferred to Haulter High School, at 1200 Sutter Street. The Wellston High School building is vacant but still standing.
Grades: 9-12
Enrollment: 432 students in 1961
Mascot: " Fighting Trojans"
School Colors: red and black
School Paper: "flashlight"
School Yearbook: "WELLHISCO"

West County Technical High School

Date Founded: 1982
Location: 13480 S. Outer 40 Drive in Chesterfield
School Architecture: two-story, contemporary, brick building
School Namesake: named for location in St. Louis County

School History: West County Technical High School opened in 1982 as one of the technical schools operated by St. Louis County Special School District. From 1987 to 1992, the technical school closed, and the facility was used for special education students. The school reopened as a technical high school and then closed in 2002. In 2003, the facility and property were purchased for the new location of Westminster Christian Academy.
Grades: 9-12
Mascot: "Falcons"
School Colors: blue and white
School Paper: none
School Yearbook: none

Yeatman High School

Date Founded: September 1904
Location: 3616 N. Garrison Avenue between Natural Bridge and Palm Street, in St. Louis City's Fairgrounds Park neighborhood
Land Cost: $35,000 in 1902
Architect: William B. Ittner
School Architecture: The ornate, three-story, all-brick building has towers on either side of the main entrance.
Building Cost: $307,766, exclusive of electric wiring, heating, plumbing and furnishings

School Namesake: James E. Yeatman (1818-1901), first president of the Mercantile Library, co-founder of the Western Sanitary Commission, businessman and philanthropist
Site History: In February 1902, the property purchased for the school had a frontage of 297 feet on the east side of Garrison Avenue between Natural Bridge and Palm Street.
School History: Yeatman High School
Yeatman High School opened as a coeducational, public high school in September 1904. The high school was renamed "Central High" in 1928. Central High provided education for grades 9-12 from 1927 to 1984. In 1984, Central High became a magnet school and was renamed "Central Visual and Performing Arts High School," which continues to provide a specialized art education for grades 9-12.
Grades: 9-12
School Yearbook: "Yeatman Life"
Alumni: Captain Hillenkoetter, who welcomed General Douglas MacArthur onboard the Battleship "Missouri" to sign the terms with the Japanese to end World War II; artist/architect Charles Eames; Mary Wickes, actress (also attended Beaumont and Hadley)

Parochial High Schools

Academy of the Sacred Heart

Date Founded: 1818
Location: 619 North Second Street, St Charles
School Namesake: named after the Society of the Sacred Heart religious order
School History: On August 29, 1769, Rose Philippine Duchesne was born in Grenoble, France, one of 12 children of wealthy parents. She was educated in a French monastery, and at the age of 18 became a nun. During the French Revolution, when Catholicism was outlawed, she joined the Society of the Sacred Heart religious order. Working through the order, she started girls' schools in Grenoble and Paris. In 1818, at the request of Bishop Louis DuBourg of New Orleans, Philippine and four other Sacred Heart nuns journeyed to New Orleans, and then up the Mississippi River to St. Charles, arriving August 21, 1818. In September, they opened the first free school west of the Mississippi; a few weeks later, they opened a tuition-based academy for girls. In 1827, Rose Philippine Duchesne opened the Academy of the Sacred Heart in St. Louis. The academy was the City's first orphanage for girls. In 1919, the nuns were transferred to Florissant, where they built new schools and a novitiate for nuns to study. In 1961, the academy had elementary students as well as approximately 100 high school students. In 1972, the high school was closed but the elementary school remained open and, for the first time, boys were admitted to the school, which is still open.

Academy of the Sacred Heart (*also see* City House)

Date Founded: 1827
Location: Taylor Avenue and Pershing Place (formerly Berlin)
Land Cost: $60,300 for 6.5 acres in 1880
School Namesake: named after the Society of the Sacred Heart religious order
School History: On August 29, 1769, Rose Philippine Duchesne was born in Grenoble, France, one of 12 children of wealthy parents. She was educated in a French monastery, and at the age of 18 became a nun. During the French Revolution, when Catholicism was outlawed, she joined the Society of the Sacred Heart religious order. Working through the order, she started girls' schools in Grenoble and Paris. In 1818, at the request of Bishop Louis DuBourg of New Orleans, Philippine and four other Sacred Heart nuns journeyed to New Orleans, and then up the Mississippi River to St. Charles, arriving August 21, 1818. In September, they opened the first free school west of the Mississippi; a few weeks later, they opened a tuition-based academy. In 1827, Rose Philippine Duchesne opened the Academy of the Sacred Heart in St. Louis. The academy was the City's first orphanage for girls. In 1919, the nuns were transferred to Florissant, where they built new schools and a novitiate for nuns to study. In 1968, the Academy of the Sacred Heart in St. Louis merged with Villa Duchesne.
Alumnae: Kate Chopin, writer

Assumption High School

Date Founded: 1948 approximately
Location: Kingshighway and Route 50 in East St. Louis City
School Architecture: contemporary, all-brick, two-story building
School Namesake: named for the assumption of Mary into heaven
School History: Assumption High School was founded in 1953 as a Catholic high school for boys, supervised by the Marianist order of priests and brothers. It was located in East St. Louis, Illinois, directly across the Mississippi River from the City of St. Louis. The first students transferred from Central Catholic High School when that school closed in 1953. (Central Catholic High School began in 1929 in St. Patrick Elementary School and was located at 6th and Illinois.) In 1974, the all-girls' St. Theresa Academy closed, and its students transferred to Assumption High School, which then became a coed Catholic high school. When Assumption High School closed in 1989, its students transferred to Althoff Catholic High School in Belleville, Illinois. The building that once housed Assumption High School currently is used as a minimum-security prison.
Mascot: "Pioneer"

School Colors: red and gold
School Yearbook: "The Pioneer"
Alumni: Dick Durbin, U. S. senator from Illinois; Jerry Costello, U. S. congressman from Illinois

Augustinian Academy for Boys

Date Founded: 1961
Location: 2900 Meramec Street; Minnesota Avenue, Osceola Street and Nebraska bounded the 21-acre tract of land where the school was located, in St. Louis City's Marquette-Cherokee neighborhood.
Site History: Maryville College of the Sacred Heart had used the location since 1872, during which time it was also an academy for boarding students and, beginning in 1882, a parish school for girls.
School History: Augustinian Academy for Boys opened in 1961, in the Maryville College facility in the Marquette-Cherokee area, when Maryville moved to St. Louis County. Augustinian Academy was managed by the Order of St. Augustine and closed in 1972; the building was demolished after a fire in 1973. Maryville Gardens apartment project is now located at that site.
Grades: 9-12

Barat Hall for Boys

Date Founded: 1913
Location: between Maryland and Pershing (formerly Berlin) Avenues at Taylor
Architect: J. H. McNamara, original architect and contractor. Hellmuth and Hellmuth designed the new wing to "City House" in 1908; it included the classrooms for Barat Hall, the new boys' school.
School Architecture: The school was a large, red brick and stone, "U"-shaped building in institutional style that was a simplified Second Empire, with Wren spire. The grand turreted entrance resembled the Governor's Palace at Williamsburg, Virginia.
Site History: The Sisters of the Sacred Heart purchased 6.5 acres for the Sisters of the Good Shepherd. The land was bounded by Taylor, Berlin (now Pershing), and Maryland Avenues and was next to the property where St. Louis notable David R. Francis built his grand house.
School History: City House was established in St. Louis City on Broadway at Convent Street in 1827 by Mother Philippine Duchesne, a religious of the Society of the Sacred Heart. In addition to an academy for young ladies, it included a convent, an orphanage, and a free school. It thrived until the mid-1880s, when the enrollment declined because the neighborhood had deteriorated. In September 1883, the sisters opened a magnificent new school facility to 115 female students on Taylor Avenue. In 1908, a new addition was built, and the nuns established the first private, Catholic boys' school in St. Louis, "Barat Hall." Because of fiscal problems, location, and the fact that the building needed extensive renovation, City House and Barat Hall closed May 28, 1968, and City House merged with Villa Duchesne in St. Louis County. Barat Hall reopened in Chesterfield and then closed.
Alumni: Tom Dooley, doctor, author and philanthropist; Joseph M. Darst, mayor of St. Louis (1949-1953)

Bishop DuBourg High School

Date Founded: 1950
Location: 5850 Eichelberger, South St. Louis City
Architect: Murphy and Mackey
School Architecture: Two-story, contemporary, all-brick building designed for 2,000 students
Building Cost: $3,000,000
School Namesake: Bishop DuBourg, selected by Mother Borgia Springrose, Superior General of the O'Fallon Sisters of the Most Precious Blood
Site History: an empty lot where kids played ball
School History: Bishop DuBourg High School was founded in 1950 and was located in a remodeled

barracks building at 67 East Sherman Road at Jefferson Barracks, in Lemay, until the new school opened in 1954. The Sisters of the Most Precious Blood of O'Fallon staffed the school. The school on Eichelberger opened in south St. Louis in January 18, 1954. It is a coeducational, Archdiocesan Catholic high school.

Grades: 9-12
Current Enrollment: approximately 612 students
Mascot: "Cavalier" and "TLGE"
School Colors: Scarlet red and white
School Paper: "Valentinian;" first year "The Cavalier"
School Yearbook: "The Cavalier"
Phone Number: 314-832-3030
Website: http://www.info@dubourg.org

Block Yeshiva High School

Date Founded: 1977
Location: 829 North Hanley - boys; 1138 N. Warson Road - girls
School Namesake: The name of the founders, Louis and Sarah Block; and "Yeshiva," meaning "House of Study" in Hebrew.
School History: The school began in the Olivette Community Center in 1977 and moved to its present facility in the early 1990s. Louis and Sarah Block founded Block Yeshiva High School. Yeshiva High School began in 1977 when a group of concerned parents and community leaders recognized the need for high-quality, traditional Jewish education combined with college preparatory general education.

Grades: 9-12
Current Enrollment: approximately 55 students
School Colors: gold and black
School Yearbook: name changes yearly
Phone Number: Boys' phone is 314-721-6390. Girls' school phone is 314-872-8701
Website: http://info.csd.org/schools/byhs/htmfiles/mail_txt.htm

Cardinal Ritter High School (1st location)

Date Founded: August 25, 1979
Location: 5421 Thekla, St. Louis City
School Namesake: Joseph Elmer Cardinal Ritter
School History: Cardinal Ritter High School opened August 25, 1979, as an Archdiocesan Catholic high school for boys. The school used the facilities that were previously Laboure and DeAndreis High School. Later, Cardinal Ritter High School became a coeducational high school. In 2003, the school moved to a new location at 701 North Spring near Grand Avenue.
Grades: 9-12

Cardinal Ritter High School (2nd location)

Date Founded: August 25, 2003
Location: 701 North Spring, near Grand Avenue in St. Louis City
Architect: Robert G. Drucker of Christner, Inc.
School Architecture: two-story, brick building with

rectangular shape and an arch over the entrance
Building Cost: $32,000,000
School Namesake: Joseph Elmer Cardinal Ritter
School History: Cardinal Ritter High School
Cardinal Ritter High School was a Catholic high school for boys that opened August 25, 1979, at 5421 Thekla in St. Louis City. The school used the facilities that were previously Laboure and DeAndreis High School. The new Cardinal Ritter High School, a coeducational, Archdiocesan, college preparatory high school, opened August 25, 2003, at its new location at 701 N. Spring in the Grand Prairie neighborhood, just west of Grand Avenue near St. Louis University. The school was built to accommodate 400 students and occupies 16.6 acres. Robert G. Drucker of Christner, Inc., was the architect and design principal on the project. The modest architectural style is based on solid aesthetic principles exhibiting quality based upon clarity and simplicity. The Archdiocesan Catholic all boys' high school replaced the old school building at 5421 Thekla Avenue in the Walnut Park neighborhood of St. Louis.
Grades: 9-12
Current Enrollment: 320 coeducational students
Mascot: "Lion"
School Colors: maroon and white
School Paper: "Ritter Journal"
School Yearbook: "Cardinal Ritter Yearbook"
Phone Number: 314-446-5500
Website: http://www.cardinalritterprep.org/index.php

Carmelite Monastery

Date Founded: 1878
Location: Soulard, on 18th Street between Victor and Sidney Streets
School History: The Carmelite Monastery was built in 1878 and was one of the first cloistered Carmelite communities in America. The three-story building originally housed approximately 21 nuns who prayed and did chores. As the Soulard area grew and became more congested, the nuns moved to a more peaceful location. In 1928, they moved to their present location in Ladue, and the Soulard location became a retreat house. In the 1950s, the original Monastery became the Little Flower Nursing Home. In 2003, Amy and Amrit Gill purchased the home for $350,000. They plan to spend $4,000,000 converting the 27,000-square foot facility into an apartment complex with 22 apartments.

Chaminade College Preparatory School

Date Founded: 1910
Location: 425 South Lindbergh Boulevard, in Central/ West St. Louis County
Land Cost: $20,000
Architect: Victor K. Klutho
School Architecture: Three-story, all-brick building with French lines and ornamentation
Building Cost: $118,800
School Namesake: Father William Joseph Chaminade, founder of the Marianist order of priests and brothers
Site History: Andrew Mitchell was granted the property in 1831. He sold it to Jesse Tailor, who sold it to James Jones, who then sold it to Samuel Denny in 1834. In 1877, Denny sold the property to a Mr. Wilkerson, who sold it to John Ghio in 1879. He, in turn, sold it to James Hazard in 1883, who sold it to McDonald in 1985 for $6,050. That same year, Hazard repurchased the property for $6,587. He built a farmhouse on it, added six more acres to the property, and sold it to the Spelbrinks in 1892 for $12,000. Although the farmhouse moved to another location on the property, it is still used as a

home by a member of the Chaminade faculty.
School History: Chaminade College Preparatory School is private, Catholic, young men's high school. The Society of Mary (Marianists) purchased the property from the Spelbrink family after appeals that were resolved by the Missouri Supreme Court on May 13, 1908. Mrs. Spelbrink, a devout Lutheran, reportedly had objected to the sale of the property to a Catholic organization. Ground was broken on May 11, 1909, and the building was completed in 1910.
Grades: 6-12
Current Enrollment: 945 high school students
Mascot: Red Devils
School Colors: Cardinal red and white
School Motto: *Esto Vir,* which means "Be a man"
School Paper: "Cardinal and White"
School Yearbook: "Cardinal and White"
Phone Number: 314-993-4400
Website: http://www.chaminademo.com

Christian Academy of Greater St. Louis

Date Founded: September 1975
Location: 11050 N. Warson Road in St. Louis County
School Namesake: a group of churches in the St. Louis area selected the name
Site History: Former Mount Pleasant Elementary School in Pattonville
School History: The Christian Academy of Greater St. Louis is a coeducational school founded in September 1975 by a group of churches in the St. Louis area. The first high school class graduated in 1976. The National Christian Schools have accredited the school.
Grades: K - 12th grade
Current Enrollment: 101 high school students
Mascot: "Crusaders"
School Colors: maroon and white with an accent of silver
School Paper: "CA Times" and quarterly "Vision"
School Yearbook: "Crusaders"
Phone Number: 314-429-7070
Website: http://www.cagsl.com

Christian Brothers College High School (Early locations)

Date Founded: 1850
Location: 6501 Clayton Road, Clayton
School Namesake: Christian Brothers who founded the school
Site History: $50,000 Easton Avenue site
School History: The Brothers of the Christian Schools founded the all boys' Catholic high school in 1850. For almost 30 years, it was located in St. Louis City at Eighth and Cerre Streets. In 1855, the State of Missouri granted the school a college charter. In 1882, the school moved to a new building at Kingshighway and Easton (now Dr. Martin Luther King) in the Arlington neighborhood. The new facility was a large, four-story building, built in the 19th-century classical style, with a curved mansard roof in the shape of a cross. On October 5, 1916, a terrible fire destroyed the building and took the lives of two of the brothers, seven firemen, and a school watchman. After the fire, the students attended school in the vacant Smith Academy on Cabanne, which was loaned to them by Washington University. Later, a new school was built. The school reopened as a high school in 1922 at 6501 Clayton Road, just northwest of Forest Park. In 2002-2003, a new school was built, and, in the fall of 2003, the school relocated to West St. Louis County. The name of the mascot changed in 1934 from "Highlander" to "Cadet" when an ROTC military program was introduced to the school. The program remained until 1993.
Mascot: "Highlander;" and beginning 1934, "Cadet"

Website: http://www.cbc-stl.org
Alumni: Robert Burnes, St. Louis newspaper sports reporter

Christian Brothers College High School (4th location)

Date Founded: 2003
Location: 1850 De LaSalle Drive, St. Louis County
Land Cost: donated
Architect: Mackey Mitchell
School Architecture: contemporary design with turrets that symbolize those from CBC on Clayton Road
Building Cost: $45,000,000
School Namesake: named for the Christian Brothers who founded the school
Site History: Novelly Estate
School History: Christian Brothers College High School (CBC) opened in August 2003 at its new location in St. Louis County (Town and County, north of Highway 40 and west of Interstate 270). The 240,000-square-foot facility is located on 24.7 acres of land plus 20 plus acres of practice fields. Approximately one-half of the cost was covered by the sale of the old Christian Brothers College High School located in Clayton. The three-story school has modest architectural style anchored by a pair of turrets that remind one of the earlier building on Clayton Road.
Grades: 9-12
Current Enrollment: approximately 1,000 students
Mascot: "Cadet"
School Colors: purple and gold
School Paper: "Turret"
School Yearbook: "Guidion"
Phone Number: 314-985-6100
Website: http://www.cbchs.org
Alumni: Mike Shannon, sportscaster, former Cardinals baseball player; Larry Hughes, NBA basketball player; Mike Peters, Pulitzer Prize-winning cartoonist

Christian Orphans Home

Date Founded: 1887
Location: 3033 North Euclid Avenue
School History: The Christian Orphans Home was founded by the Christian Church and was located at 1335 Bayard Avenue in the Fairgrounds neighborhood. In 1900, the home moved to 915 Aubert Avenue. In 1907, it moved to its present location at 3033 North Euclid Avenue. In 1923, the home was enlarged and changed its name to "St. Louis Christian Home."

City House

Date Founded: 1893
Location: East side of Taylor Avenue between Maryland and Berlin (now Pershing) Avenues
Land Cost: $60,300 in 1880
Architect: J. H. McNamara, original architect and contractor. Hellmuth and Hellmuth designed the new wing in 1908; it included the classrooms for Barat Hall, the new boys' school.
School Architecture: The school was a large, red brick and stone, "U"-shaped building in institutional style that was a simplified Second Empire, with Wren spire. The grand entrance resembled the Governor's Palace at Williamsburg, Virginia.
School Namesake: the City of St. Louis
Site History: Sisters of the Sacred Heart purchased 6.5 acres for the Sisters of the Good Shepherd. The land was bounded by Taylor, Berlin (now Pershing), and Maryland Avenues and was next to the property where former mayor David R. Francis built his grand house.
School History: City House was established in St. Louis City on Broadway at Convent Street in

1827 by Mother Philippine Duchesne, a religious of the Society of the Sacred Heart. In addition to an academy for young ladies, it included a convent, an orphanage, and a free school. It thrived until the mid-1880s, when the enrollment declined because the neighborhood had deteriorated. In September 1883, the Sisters opened a magnificent new school facility to 115 female students on Taylor Avenue. In 1908, a new addition was built, and the nuns established the first private, Catholic boys' school in St. Louis, "Barat Hall." Because of the economy, location, and the fact that it required extensive renovation, City House closed May 28, 1968, and merged with Villa Duchesne in St. Louis County. Barat Hall reopened in Chesterfield.
Grades: 9-12

Concordia Seminary

Date Founded: prior to 1888
Location: 801 DeMun Avenue in Clayton
School Architecture: Gothic-style, stone buildings with a central tower and multiple quadrangles on a 72-acre campus
School History: Concordia Seminary began as Concordia College, located on Jefferson Avenue in St. Louis City. It was a large, ornate, brick, three-story building with a large Gothic tower located above the entrance and wings on both sides. The college was devoted to the preparation of young men for the ministry who had taken regular courses at other colleges or schools, especially those belonging to the German Evangelical Lutheran denomination. The current seminary is open to individuals interested in serving in the Lutheran pastoral ministry, including high school-age men. Recently, the Seminary purchased the Christian Brothers College High School on Clayton Road. The facility was vacated when the new high school was built in West County and the students transferred there in 2003.
Phone Number: 314-505-7000 (314-505-7722 high school youth)
Website: http://www.csl.edu

Cor Jesu Academy

Date Founded: 1956
Location: 10230 Gravois Road, Affton
School Architecture: single-story, brick, contemporary building
School Namesake: *Cor Jesu* means "Heart of Jesus"
Site History: reportedly a stop on the "Underground Railroad" and a Civil War-era home
School History: Cor Jesu Academy is a private, all-girls' Catholic high school that was established in 1956 and has been at its present location near Grant's Farm since 1965. The school is owned and operated by the Apostles of the Sacred Heart of Jesus.
Grades: 9-12
Current Enrollment: approximately 545 female students
Mascot: "Charger"
School Colors: red and white
School Paper: "Corette"
School Yearbook: "Corde"
Distinguished Awards: Blue Ribbon School by the United States Department of Education
Phone Number: 314-842-1546
Website: http://www.corjesu.pvtK12.mo.us
Alumnae: Ann Trusdale Wagner, co-chairman of the National Republican Party

Corpus Christi High School

Date Founded: 1953
Location: 2100 Switzer Avenue in Jennings
School Namesake: *Corpus Christi* means "Body of Jesus"

School History: Corpus Christi High School was a Catholic parish high school for girls established in 1953; it was staffed by diocesan priests and Ursuline Sisters of the Roman Union and lay teachers. The school closed in 1973.
Grades: 9-12

Coyle High School
Date Founded: 1939
Location: Clay Avenue in Kirkwood
School Architecture: two-story, brick, rectangular building with a peaked façade over the entrance
School Namesake: Father Eugene Coyle
Site History: Adams Public School
School History: Coyle High School opened in 1939 as a parish Catholic high school, built on the site of Adams Public School in Kirkwood. It was purchased from the City of Kirkwood by St. Peter's parish. The coeducational high school was located on Clay Avenue and was named in honor of Father Eugene Coyle. The Ursuline Sisters taught the girls, and the Brothers of the Society of Mary taught the boys. The school served elementary and high school students from St. Peter's and other local parishes. Coyle High School closed in June 1960. The building was then used as a grade school for St. Peter's parish. In 1960, the high school's male students transferred to the new St. John Vianney High School, and the girls transferred to Ursuline Academy.

DeAndreis Catholic High School
Date Founded: 1942
Location: 4275 Clarence, in St. Louis
School Namesake: named in honor of Rev. Felix DeAndreis, an early St. Louis Catholic educator
School History: DeAndreis Catholic High School began in 1948 as for boys; it was located in a facility at Switzer and Jennings. DeAndreis was operated by the Brothers of Mary and was named in honor of Rev. Felix DeAndreis, an early St. Louis Catholic educator. In 1947, DeAndreis High School for boys moved to a new building at 4275 Clarence Avenue. In 1952, DeAndreis became coeducational and remained that way until 1963, when it reverted back to a high school for boys. In 1976, the school closed because of declining enrollment. From 1976 to 1992, the St. Louis School District used the facility, conducting classes there for the Academy of Mathematics and Science.
Grades: 9-12

DeSmet Jesuit High School
Date Founded: 1967
Location: 233 North New Ballas Road, Creve Coeur
Architect: Stander and Sons
School Architecture: Contemporary
School Namesake: Father Pierre DeSmet, a missionary to the Indians of the Western Plains and Pacific Northwest
Site History: farmland
School History: DeSmet Jesuit High School opened in 1967 and is a private, Catholic, all-male high school, run by the Jesuits (Society of Jesus).

Grades: 9-12
Current Enrollment: approximately 1,225 male students
Mascot: "Spartans"
School Colors: maroon and white
School Paper: "Mirror"
School Yearbook: "Odyssey"
Phone Number: 314-567-3500
Website: http://www.admissions@desmet.org
Alumni: Judge Henry Autry, federal judge; Frank Cusumano, St. Louis TV sportscaster; Chris Higgins, KTVI-TV meteorologist

Duchesne High School

Date Founded: 1924
Location: 2550 Elm Street in St. Charles
School Architecture: contemporary, all-brick, one-story building
School Namesake: St. Rose Phillipine Duchesne
School History: Duchesne High School is a Catholic, regional, coeducational high school. It was established as St. Peter High School for young women in 1924 and became coed prior to 1940. The high school remained at St. Peter Parish until 1956, when the school moved to its current location and changed its name to Duchesne High School.
Grades: 9-12
Current Enrollment: approximately 720 students
Mascot: "Pioneers"
School Colors: blue and white
School Paper: "Trailblazer"
School Yearbook: "Cor Duchesne"
Phone Number: 636-946-6767
Website: http:// www.duchesne-hs.org

Eden Seminary

Date Founded: 1858
Location: 475 East Lockwood Avenue Webster Groves
School Architecture: gothic-style towers and six buildings in a campus setting on 20 acres
School Namesake: Eden Station in Normandy
School History: In 1858, the college of the German Evangelical Synod of North America for the education of ministers moved from Femme Osage, in Warren County, Missouri, to St. Louis County. The college was located on St. Charles Rock Road and Hunt Avenue, just opposite Eden Station on the Wabash Railroad. The ornate, four-story, brick building with four frontal cupolas and a central tower could accommodate 100 students at a time. In 1923, the expanding Normandy School District purchased Eden Seminary for $200,000 and in the 1923 –1924 school year shared the facilities and maintenance expenses. After that year, Eden Seminary moved to its present location in Webster Groves.
Phone Number: 314-961-3627
Website: http://www.eden.edu

Edgewood Children's Center

Date Founded: 1834
Location: 330 North Gore, Webster Groves
School Namesake: "Edgewood" named by residents – center is near the edge of the woods
Site History: The Edgewood Children's Center is currently located in a building (formerly Stone House, then Rock House) constructed in 1850 by Artimus Bullard, an abolitionist and minister. Originally, it was a secondary school for young men interested in religious life.
School History: The home began in 1834 as the St. Louis Association for Relief of Orphan Children, then St. Louis Protestant Orphans' Asylum, then St. Louis Protestant Orphans Home. It was created in response to the 1832 cholera epidemic, which left many St. Louis children without parents. In 1853, the Girls' Industrial School was formed to care for and educate vagrant girls; in time, the school merged with Edgewood. In 1865, the home merged with the Soldiers Orphan Home of Webster Groves, which was established to address problems caused by the Civil War. In 1943, it became Edgewood Children's Center. In 1978, Edgewood merged with the Girls' Industrial Home and School. The school was founded as the Girls' Industrial School in 1853 as a learning center for poverty-stricken girls. It evolved into a treatment center for girls with psychiatric problems who received assistance form the Municipal Psychiatric Clinic and Child Guidance Clinic. In the early days, the children attended off-grounds schools. Today the students wear uniforms and attend classes on grounds. The school provides education for young boys and girls with behavioral, communication and emotional problems.

Grades: 3 years - 17 years
Current Enrollment: approximately 40 resident students and 100 daytime students
Phone Number: 314-968-2060
Website: http://www.eccstl.org

Epworth Children and Family Services

Date Founded: 1909
Location: 110 North Elm Avenue, Webster Groves
School History: Epworth School for Girls began when German-speaking Methodists founded the Central Wesleyan Orphans' Home in 1864 in Warrenton, Missouri, to care for Civil War orphans. The next year, a Methodist layman founded an orphanage in St. Louis. The home was a project of the Methodists (Episcopal Church, South) of Eastern Missouri and, in 1867, it was called the "Methodist Orphan's Home." In 1939, the Central Wesleyan Orphans' Home merged with the Methodist Orphan's Home and became the Methodist Children's Home for Boys on Jamieson. Epworth School for Girls was founded in 1909 and was located in St. Louis City. On December 2, 1922, the home moved to Webster Groves. In 1975, the current Epworth Home was created with the merger of the Methodist Children's Home and Epworth School for Girls.
Phone Number: 314-961-5718
Website: http://www.epworthchildrenshome.org

Evangelical Children's Home

Date Founded: 1858
Location: 8240 St. Charles Rock Road, St. Louis County
School Namesake: named for the religion of the founder
Site History: farm
School History: The home was founded by Reverend Louis Edward Nollau on January 20, 1858, when he began a shelter for orphans at his church on Carr Street in St. Louis. It originally was named the "German Protestant Orphan's Home" because it cared for children placed there after they were found roaming the streets and sleeping in doorways following recurrent outbreaks of cholera. In the fall of 1866, the Home moved to a farm on St. Charles Rock Road, where the current campus is still located. The Home continues to accept and care for children but for different reasons than when the Home was founded. Most of children in the Home now have suffered severe physical, sexual, and emotional abuse and neglect. In 2001, a new school facility was built that was funded entirely by donations.
Grades: 4th through 12th
Current Enrollment: approximately 38 high school students
Mascot: "Tigers"
School Colors: black and gold
Phone Number: 314-427-3755
Website: http://www.newbeginnings-Ech.org

Gateway Academy of Chesterfield

Date Founded: 1992
Location: 7815 Wild Horse Creek Road, St. Louis County
Architect: Jack Tyrer
School Architecture: contemporary, red brick, single- and two-story building
School History: Gateway Academy is a coeducational, Catholic school founded in 1992 by a group of lay leaders in association with the Legionaries of Christ. To accommodate its growth, the high school opened its present campus in Chesterfield in 1999.
Grades: Pre-K to 12
Current Enrollment: approximately 80 high school students

Mascot: "Titans"
School Colors: blue and gold
School Paper: "The Titan"
School Yearbook: "Gateway Academy"
Phone Number: 636-519-9099
Website: http:// www.gatewayacademy.org

Incarnate Word Academy

Date Founded: 1932
Location: 2788 Normandy Drive, north St. Louis County
School Architecture: multiple, contemporary-style, brick buildings
Site History: Lucas Estate and St. Vincent Park
School History: Incarnate Word Academy was founded as a private, Catholic high school for girls by the Sisters of Charity of the Incarnate Word.
Grades: 9-12
Current Enrollment: approximately 540 female students
Mascot: ""Red Knights"
School Colors: red and gold
School Paper: "The Word for Word"
School Yearbook: title changes yearly
Phone Number: 314-725-5850
Website: http://www.iwacademy.org
Alumni: Linda Behlmann, of Behlmann Motors; Shandi Finnessey, Miss USA 2004

Kain High School

Date Founded: 1911
Location: St. Teresa's Parish
School Namesake: Archbishop of St. Louis, John Joseph Kain
School History: Students attending Kain High School at St. Teresa's Parish were taught by the Sisters of St. Joseph. By 1917, Rosati and Kain high schools were so crowded that they combined and moved into the three-story St. Vincent's Seminary on Grand and Lucas. The facility was available because the Daughters of Charity closed their "select" school in order to conform to their vocation to serve the poor. In 1919, the school property was sold, and the Hayes mansion at Lindell and Newstead was purchased for the new school. In September 1922, the school was relocated to a new, three-story, classical, sand-colored brick building at 4389 Lindell Boulevard. In 1945, the student enrollment peaked to 1,080 students. The first black students began attending the school in 1947.
Grades: 9-12

John F. Kennedy Catholic High School

Date Founded: 1968
Location: 500 Woods Mill Road, Manchester
School Architecture: one- and two-story, contemporary brick building
School Namesake: John F. Kennedy, first Catholic president of the United States
School History: John F. Kennedy High School was founded in 1968. It is West County's only coeducational, Archdiocesan Catholic high school.
Grades: 9-12
Current Enrollment: approximately 525 male and female students
Mascot: "Celts" (*a.k.a.* Fin McCool)
School Colors: green and gold

School Paper: "Torch"
School Yearbook: "Profiles"
Phone Number: 636-227-5900
Website: http:// www.jfk-catholic-high.org
Alumni: Bob Burnes (Paving Company)

Kenrick High School

Date Founded: 1911
Location: Leffingwell Avenue and Locust Street
School Namesake: Cardinal Peter Richard Kenrick
School History: Kenrick High School was opened on August 18, 1911, as the first Archdiocesan High School for boys in the City of St. Louis. It was located in the school building of Saints Peter and Paul Parish, which operated a parochial high school. The Brothers of Mary ran the new high school; initial enrollment was 65 boys. In 1913, the school relocated to a facility at Leffingwell Avenue and Locust Streets; by 1915, enrollment had increased to 137 boys. When Kenrick High School closed in 1925, the 500 students transferred to the new McBride High School on Kingshighway.
Grades: 9-12

Kenrick-Glennon Seminary

Date Founded: 1818
Location: 5200 Glennon
School Namesake: Cardinal Peter Richard Kenrick and Cardinal Glennon
Site History: *see below*
School History: The Vincentians established St. Mary's of the Barrens Seminary in Perryville, Missouri in 1818. In 1842, the St. Louis diocesan Major Seminary opened on Carroll Street in the Soulard area of south St. Louis, and older Perryville students were transferred there. A

year and a half later, the Seminary relocated to the Vincentian-owned Soulard Mansion on Decatur Street; in 1848, it moved to Carondelet. In 1858, both the St. Louis Major Seminary in Carondelet and the Perryville Minor Seminary were transferred to Cape Girardeau. On September 21, 1893, the new Kenrick Seminary opened in a former convent at 19th and Cass Avenue. In 1915, the facilities were deemed inadequate, and a second Kenrick Seminary was opened on Kenrick Road in what later became Shrewsbury. Since 1987, this second Kenrick Seminary has been known as the Archdiocesan Pastoral Center. As the second Kenrick opened, the Minor Seminary moved to a new location at 4244 Washington Avenue. In 1927, a tornado extensively damaged this location, and the Minor Seminary was moved temporarily to St. Bridget's Parish on Jefferson Avenue and Stoddard Street while the facility was rebuilt. In 1931, the first St. Louis Preparatory Seminary, the present Kenrick-Glennon Seminary building, opened on the same grounds as the second Kenrick. This facility housed the last two years of high school. The first two years of high school were reinstated at the refurbished Washington Avenue location, now known as the Cathedral Latin School. In 1947, the Latin School was closed and six-year programs were established in the two Archdiocesan seminaries. Prep comprised four years of high school and two years of college; Kenrick comprised two years of college and four years of theology. In 1957, a new high school facility was opened at 5200 Shrewsbury Avenue on the same grounds as Kenrick and the old Prep. The education facilities were reallocated: the new Prep became the four-year high school, and the old Prep, a four-year college that became known as Cardinal Glennon College. Kenrick continued as a four-year theologate. In 1965, increasing enrollment led to the creation of the "new Prep," St. Louis Preparatory Seminary North (counterpart to Prep in Shrewsbury, called "Prep South"). It began in the basement of Sacred Heart School Building on North Jefferson in Florissant and moved to 3500 St. Catherine in Florissant. St. Louis Preparatory Seminary North was closed in the spring of 1987 because of declining enrollment, and the two high school seminaries were amalgamated at the facility in Shrewsbury, once again becoming known as St. Louis Preparatory Seminary. In

May 1991, the high school seminary closed. Cardinal Glennon Seminary is still operating as a postgraduate, freestanding school in Theology.
Grades: 9-12
Phone Number: 314-644-0266

Laboure High School

Date Founded: 1942
Location: 5421 Thekla, St. Louis City
School History: Laboure High School was founded in 1942 by the Daughters of Charity as a Catholic high school for girls known as "North Side High School." North Side High School became "Laboure High School" in 1948. In 1952, Laboure became a coeducational high school, and it remained so until 1965, when it reverted back to a high school for girls. The school has shared a five-acre campus with St. Mary's Orphan Home, and then in 1952 with St. Mary's Special School for Exceptional Children. Laboure High School closed in 1979.

Loretto Academy

Date Founded: 1847
Location: near the terminus of the Western, Cable and Narrow Gauge Railway, on Lafayette (now Pillar Place), Florissant
School Architecture: Stately, four-story, all-brick building with a mansard roof
School Namesake: named for the Sisters of Loretto
Site History: located a few hundred feet southwest of St. Ferdinand's Church
School History: The Sisters of Loretto in Florissant founded Loretto Academy, also known as "Young Ladies' Academy," in 1847. Situated on several acres with shaded walks and groves of trees, it had an elegant chapel, parlors, various study and music halls, two recreational halls for seniors and juniors, and an exhibition hall that could accommodate more than 1,000 people. On January 4, 1919, the building was destroyed by fire. At that time, the academy had 50 students ranging in age from five to 15. The school closed in 1956.

Lutheran High School

Date Founded: August 25, 1946
Location: Lake and Waterman Avenues in St. Louis
School Namesake: Martin Luther
School History: Lutheran High School, founded by Dr. Paul Lang, was dedicated on August 25, 1946, and was located at Lake and Waterman Avenues in St. Louis. The school remained at that location but was renamed "Lutheran High School Central" in 1957, when Lutheran High School South opened. The facility closed in 1965, when a new high school, "Lutheran High School North," opened at 5401 Lucas and Hunt in north St. Louis County.
Grades: 9-12
Mascot: "Crusaders"
School Colors: maroon and gold
School Paper: "Carrier"
School Yearbook: "Crusader"

Lutheran Central High School

Date Founded: 1946
Location: Lake and Waterman
School Namesake: Martin Luther
School History: *see* Lutheran High School
Grades: 9-12
Mascot: "Crusaders"
School Colors: maroon and gold
School Paper: "Carrier"
School Yearbook: "Crusader"

Lutheran High School North

Date Founded: 1965
Location: 5401 Lucas and Hunt in North St. Louis County
Architect: Ken Wischmeyer
School Architecture: single- and two-story, contemporary, brick, rectangular building
School Namesake: Martin Luther
Site History: site was carved out of a hill.
School History: *See above.* Lutheran North High School has a campus of 22 acres bounded by Norwood Country Club on two sides, Memorial Park Cemetery, and an apartment complex. A recent acquisition of 27 acres increased the school site to 50 acres and now provides frontage on Interstate 70, so the athletic fields can be seen from that highway.
Grades: 9-12
Current Enrollment: approximately 381 students
Mascot: "Crusaders"
School Colors: maroon and gold
School Paper: "Currier"
School Yearbook: "Crusader"
Phone Number: 314-389-3100
Website: http://www.lhsn.org
Alumni: Steve Atwater, Denver Broncos NFL football team; Kurt Peterson, Dallas Cowboys NFL football team

Lutheran High School South

Date Founded: 1957
Location: 9515 Tesson Ferry Road, St. Louis County
School Architecture: single- and two-story, contemporary, brick, rectangular building
School Namesake: Martin Luther
School History: Lutheran South High School was founded in 1957.
Grades: 9-12
Current Enrollment: 613 students
Mascot: "Lancers"
School Colors: black and gold
School Paper: "Troubadour"
School Yearbook: "Lance"
Phone Number: 314-631-1400
Website: http://www.lhssonline.org

McBride High School

Date Founded: January 5, 1925
Location: 1909 N. Kingshighway
School Architecture: white stone, ornate, Grecian-style building with six large columns at the entrance
School Namesake: William Cullen McBride, a wealthy businessman
School History: McBride High School was established as an Archdiocesan Catholic boys' high school run by a Marianist faculty. McBride's initial enrollment of 520 students was transferred from Kenrick High School, which had closed. The school was named for William Cullen McBride, a wealthy businessman whose daughter donated money for the school. On May 23, 1971, McBride held its final open house and then closed; the facility was sold to the St.

Louis School District. Later, it became the home of Martin Luther King, Jr., High School, and then several Tri-A high schools.
Grades: 9-12
Enrollment: 520 initially
School Colors: white, green and orange; colors were those of the Irish flag
School Paper: "The Colonnade"

Mercy High School

Date Founded: 1948
Location: 1000 Pennsylvania in University City
School Namesake: named for "Our Lady of Mercy"
School History: In 1948, the Sisters of Mercy of the Union founded Mercy High School, the first Archdiocesan, coeducational high school in St. Louis County. The high school was located in University City and was staffed by the Sisters of Mercy until 1985. In 1985, Mercy High School merged with St. Thomas Aquinas High School, creating St. Thomas Aquinas-Mercy High School. The school was located on 845 Dunn Road in Florissant; it closed in 2003.
Grades: 9-12

Missouri Baptist Children's Home

Date Founded: 1886
Location: 11300 St. Charles Rock Road, St. Louis County
School Namesake: named for the religion of the founders
School History: The Missouri Baptist Children's Home, originally called the Baptist Orphan's Home, began in St. Louis City in April 1886 in a rented residence on 2652 Morgan Street with 12 rooms. The Home housed orphaned children as well as children of unwed mothers, children whose families could not provide for them, and abandoned children. In May 1887, the Home moved into a building at 1906 Lafayette Avenue in St. Louis. It remained at that location until 1907, when it moved to its present site in Bridgeton.
Phone Number: 314-738-0568
Website: http://www.mbch.org

Mount Providence School for Boys

Date Founded: 1933
Location: 8351 Florissant Road, Normandy
School Architecture: all-brick, three-story building
School Namesake: named for the Sisters of Divine Providence who founded the school, and for its location on a tall hill
School History: The Sisters of Divine Providence (CDPs) founded Mount Providence School for Boys in 1933 as a boarding school for boys; it became a day school in 1984 and coeducational in 1988. From 1956–1969, space in the building was leased to Catholic Charities' Villa Maria home for unwed mothers. The facility became a Motherhouse from 1992-1997. In 1992, "Room at the Inn" came to Mount Providence as a co-sponsored ministry for the Salvation Army; the program became fully sponsored by the CDPs in April 1993. The building was demolished on February 10, 2001, to allow the Department of Transportation to remove a dangerous curve from the Interstate and to increase the size of the University of Missouri, St. Louis campus.

Nerinx Hall High School

Date Founded: 1924
Location: 530 East Lockwood, Webster Groves
School Architecture: contemporary
School Namesake: Father Charles Nerinckx (1761-1824), founder of the Sisters Loretto Standing at the Foot of the Cross
Site History: Lockwood Estate. The Lockwoods were one of the founding families of Webster Groves.

School History: Nerinx Hall High School traces its beginning to Webster College in the early 1900s. When the State required high schools to be separate from colleges and universities, Nerinx Hall High School separated from Webster College in 1924 and became a private, Catholic girls' high school run by the Sisters of Loretto.
Grades: 9-12
Current Enrollment: approximately 600 female students
Mascot: "Hallmarker"
School Colors: green and white
School Paper: "Hallways"
School Yearbook: "The Key"
Distinguished Awards: Blue Ribbon School by the United States Department of Education
Phone Number: 314-968-1505
Website: http://www.nerinxhs.org
Alumnae: Actresses Marsha Mason and Mary Frann; Kathryn Jamboretz, KPLR-TV newswoman; Zoe Vonder Haar, St. Louis actress

North County Christian School

Location: 1309 N. Elizabeth Avenue, St. Louis County
School Namesake: location and religion
School History: North County Christian
School Grades: Pre-K to 12th
Phone Number: 314-522-6086
Website: http://www.nccsedu.org

North Side Catholic High School

Date Founded: 1942
Location: 5421 Thekla, in St. Louis City's Fairgrounds neighborhood
School Namesake: location and religion
School History: North Side High School for boys began in 1942. It later was named "DeAndreis High School," operated by the Brothers of Mary.
Grades: 9-12

Notre Dame High School

Date Founded: 1934
Location: 320 East Ripa Avenue, Lemay
Land Cost: $21,000
School Architecture: Notre Dame High School is a three-story, red brick, contemporary building
School Namesake: *Notre Dame* means "Our Lady"
Site History: Grand View Estate in 1894 (40 acres). Earlier owners of Grandview were Henry T. Blow and the Knight and DeMenil families.
School History: The School Sisters of Notre Dame (SSND), established in Germany, opened a Mother House for 100 sisters in Lemay in 1895. On July 7, 1897, the School Sisters of Notre Dame dedicated the first two wings of their Motherhouse, "Santa Maria in Ripa" (St. Mary on the Bank). At that time, they provided high school education only to young girls who lived in the Mother House and were planning to become nuns. In 1934, at the request of local families, the Sisters agreed to open a Catholic high school for girls in the community for lower- and middle-class students and built the high school next to the Mother House. These new students not planning to enter the convent were known as "day hops." Notre Dame High School opened in 1955.
Grades: 9-12
Current Enrollment: approximately 430 students
Mascot: "Rebels"
School Colors: white and blue

School Paper: "Rebel Rouser"
School Yearbook: "Rebellion"
Phone Number: 314-544-1015
Website: http://www.ndhs.net

Peter and Paul High School (*see* Kenrick High School)

(The) Principia Upper School

Date Founded: 1910
Location: 13201 Clayton Road
School Architecture: primarily single-story, contemporary, brick building
School Namesake: derived from the word "principle"
Site History: farmland
School History: The Principia began in 1898, when Mary Kimball Morgan wanted to "home school" her own children, and Christian Scientist friends convinced her to establish an elementary school in her home at 3214 Morgan Street (now Delmar). In 1901, the elementary school moved to a larger campus at Page and Belt Avenues in the Cabanne neighborhood. In 1910, the high school and a junior college were founded. In 1932, a four-year liberal arts college was founded on the Principia campus. In 1934, the senior college moved to its present campus in Elsah, Illinois. Property later was purchased on Clayton Road in west St. Louis County. In the 1950s, a school was built and the preschool students moved into the facility. In 1961, the other sections of the school moved to that location. The old campus on Page Avenue is now the Page Park Y.M.C.A.

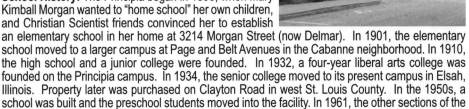

Grades: 9-12
Current Enrollment: approximately 350 male and female students
Mascot: "Panther"
School Colors: gold and blue
School Motto: "as the sowing the reaping"
School Paper: "Voice"
School Yearbook: "The Blade"
Phone Number: 314-434-2100
Website: http://www.prin.edu
Alumni: Congressman David Dreier, R-CA, chairman of the House of Representatives Rules Committee

Protestant Children's Home

Date Founded: 1877
Location: 12685 Olive Street Road, Creve Coeur
School Namesake: religion of founders
School History: German-General Protestant Orphans Home was founded in 1877, in a home near 17th and Chouteau in the Fairgrounds neighborhood. It was founded by a group of German-Americans because of a critical need to provide a safe home for orphaned children. In the late 1880s, the home moved to a more rural site on 4447 Natural Bridge Road near Newstead. It remained at that location until 1962, when it moved to its present location in Creve Coeur. It is now called the "Protestant Children's Home."

Rosary High School

Date Founded: 1961
Location: 1720 Redman Avenue, north St. Louis County
School Architecture: two-story, brick and glass, contemporary building
School Namesake: the Rosary of Mary
School History: Rosary High School was founded as an Archdiocesan Catholic, coeducational high school and was staffed by diocesan priests and the School Sisters of Notre Dame. Rosary High School closed at the end of the 2002-2003 school year; on August 21, 2003, Trinity Catholic High School opened at the site. Trinity is the result of a merger between St. Thomas Aquinas-Mercy High School on Dunn Road, in Florissant, and Rosary High School, on Redman Road in Spanish Lake, the site of the new school.
Grades: 9-12
Mascot: "Rebels"
School Colors: yellow and white
School Paper: "Rebel Yell"
School Yearbook: "Reveille"

Rosati High School

Date Founded: 1911
Location: Saints Peter and Paul Parish, in the Soulard district of St. Louis City
School Namesake: Rosati High School was named in honor of the Archbishop of St. Louis, Joseph Rosati.
School History: the School Sisters of Notre Dame taught Rosati High School students at Saints Peter and Paul Parish in the Soulard district.
Grades: 9-12

Rosati-Kain High School

Date Founded: 1912
Location: 4389 Lindell Boulevard
School Architecture: Three-story, classical, sand-colored brick building
School Namesake: Rosati-Kain High School was named in honor of two St. Louis Catholic leaders, Bishop Joseph Rosati and Archbishop John Joseph Kain.
School History: Rosati-Kain High School opened in 1912 at Grand and Lucas in the St. Vincent Seminary when two parish high schools, started in 1911, combined to form a single, Roman Catholic high school for girls in grades 9-12. Students attending Rosati High School at Saints Peter and Paul Parish in the Soulard district were taught by the School Sisters of Notre Dame, and the students attending Kain High School at St. Teresa's Parish were taught by the Sisters of St. Joseph. By 1917, the two schools were so crowded that they combined and moved into the three-story St. Vincent's Seminary on Grand and Lucas. The facility was available because the Daughters of Charity had closed their "select" school in order to conform to their vocation to serve the poor. In 1919, the school property was sold, and the Hayes mansion at Lindell and Newstead was purchased for the new school. In September 1922, the school was relocated to the address on Lindell Boulevard. In 1945, the student enrollment peaked to 1,080 students. The first black students began attending the school in 1947.
Grades: 9-12
Current Enrollment: 420 female students
Mascot: "Cougar"
School Colors: purple and gold
School Yearbook: no particular name

Phone Number: 314-533-8513
Website: http://www.rosati-kain.org

St. Alphonsus Liguori (Rock) High School

Date Founded: 1844
Location: 1204 North Grand Boulevard, St. Louis City
Architect: Reverend Louis Dold
School Namesake: St. Alphonsus Liguori
School History: St. Alphonsus Liguori "The Rock" Catholic Church was built in 1873 in an unpopulated area beyond City limits for Redemptorist missions and spiritual retreats. In 1881, because of westward expansion, its status changed to a parish church. The high school traces its origin to 1844 as a parish high school for girls that was managed by the School Sisters of Notre Dame. The high school, which was adjacent to Church, closed in 1972.
Grades: 9-12

St. Anthony of Padua High School

Date Founded: September 3, 1920
Location: 3112 Meramec Street and Michigan Avenues, St. Louis City
School Namesake: St. Anthony of Padua
School History: St. Anthony High School was founded as a parish Catholic, commercial school for girls adjacent to St. Anthony of Padua Church. In 1927, it became a four-year high school. The church is the oldest Roman Catholic Church in the Marquette-Cherokee Neighborhood. The Franciscan Fathers founded the parish in 1863 in connection with their monastery. The school closed at the end of the 1980 school year.
Grades: 9-12
Enrollment: approximately 270 girls in 1961

St. Elizabeth Academy

Date Founded: September 1, 1882
Location: 3401 Arsenal Street (formerly Susquehanna), in the Southwest neighborhood of St. Louis City's Crittenden District
Architect: Franciscan Brother Leonard Darscheid, OSM, in 1914; the new high school, Anthony Studer & Son
Architecture: contemporary; some other architectural styles for the gym
School Namesake: St. Elizabeth of Hungary
Site History: Home of Christopher Jacob Schiller, the proprietor of the Swan Tavern at the riverfront
School History: After Christopher Schiller died, his wife wanted to have a religious order open an orphanage. In the fall of 1874, the Sisters of St. Mary began living in the mansion and started the orphanage. By 1881, the order had built a small, three-story dormitory for the orphans at a cost of $25,000, but they were $14,000 in debt. Because of financial problems, a change in management was made. On September 1, 1882, six Sisters of the Most Precious Blood of O'Fallon and four students replaced the previous occupants. The eight orphans that were cared for by the Sisters of St. Mary were transferred to the Sisters of the Most Precious Blood Mother House in O'Fallon, Missouri. St. Elizabeth Academy is a private, Catholic high school for girls, founded in 1882 by the Sisters of the Most Precious Blood of O'Fallon, Missouri. It was founded for lower- and middle-class young ladies and taught Domestic Science (later called "home economics"). The first high school buildings were constructed on the site of the Schiller mansion in the 1880s and included a chapel and gymnasium. The roof of the gymnasium, built in 1927 and designed by Gustel Kiewitt, was the first lamella roof in St. Louis. The roof has a system of arches that span large areas without intermediate vertical supports. This same unique roof was used on the St. Louis Arena in 1929. In 1958-1959, a new school was built on the site, and the original gymnasium was reused for the new

school. One-half of the original chapel was retained and remodeled for the new choral room.
Current Enrollment: approximately 210 female students
Mascot: "Seahawk" (first three letters, "SEA," stand for St. Elizabeth Academy)
School Colors: red and white
School Paper: "Thuringian" (named for St. Elizabeth's home town of Thuringia in Bavaria)
School Yearbook: "Elizabethan"
Phone Number: 314-771-5134
Website: http:// www.stelizabethacademy.org
Alumni: Dr. Mary Frances Nawrocki McGinnis, first woman admitted to St. Louis University Medical School

St. Francis Borgia High School

Date Founded: 1982
School History: St. Francis Borgia High School was founded in 1982 as an Archdiocesan High School. Students were taught by Archdiocesan priests and the School Sisters of Notre Dame.

St. Francis deSales High School

Date Founded: 1939
Location: 2653 Ohio Avenue, south St. Louis
School Namesake: St. Francis deSales
School History: St. Francis deSales High School was part of St. Francis de Sales Catholic Church, located in south St. Louis. It opened as a parish, coeducational high school staffed by diocesan priests and the School Sisters of Notre Dame, filling a need for more Catholic high schools because of an increasing population. The junior high school opened in the fall of 1939 and was expanded into a high school, which had its first graduation class in 1947. The elementary school and high school were built on the site of the original St. Francis deSales elementary school, which was built in 1872 and razed in the late 1930s to make room for the new school. As the population of the City moved to the County, enrollment decreased, and the high school closed at the end of the 1973 school year. The present St. Francis deSales Catholic Church was dedicated in 1908 and is the only one in the St. Louis area that is of German Gothic architecture. It can be readily identified by its 300-foot high spire.
Grades: 9-12

St. John the Baptist High School

Date Founded: 1922
Location: 5021 Adkins Avenue, St. Louis's Bevo neighborhood
School Architecture: contemporary, two-story, rectangular, brick building
School Namesake: St. John the Baptist
Site History: The church purchased six lots on Adkins Avenue across the street from the rectory and built the high school. At the request of Father Peters, Adkins Avenue  was closed, but the school continues to have the Adkins Avenue address.
School History: St. John the Baptist College Prep High School is a parish Catholic, coeducational high school, founded in 1922 as a two-year, all-boys' commercial high school. By 1930, it had developed into a four-year, coeducational, comprehensive high school.
Grades: 9-12
Current Enrollment: approximately 320 male and female students
Mascot: "Lion"
School Colors: blue and gold
School Paper: previously "Echo;" none at present time
School Yearbook: name changes yearly
Phone Number: 314-351-5604

Website: http:// www.stjohnshigh.com

St. John Vianney High School

Date Founded: 1960
Location: 1311 South Kirkwood Road, Kirkwood
School Architecture: single-story, glass and brick, contemporary building
School Namesake: St. John Vianney
Site History: The Marianists purchased the "Brown Hurst" property and mansion in 1917. Mr. Brown was a horticulturist who bequeathed his extensive orchid collection to the Missouri Botanical Garden.
School History: St. John Vianney High School is an all boys' Catholic high school, founded in 1960 by the Society of Mary (Marianists). The first male students transferred from Coyle High School (St. Peter's Parish) when it closed in May 1960, and the first three Vianney graduating classes were former Coyle High students.
Grades: 9-12
Current Enrollment: approximately 810 students
Mascot: Golden Griffins
School Colors: black and gold
School Paper: "Griffin"
School Yearbook: "Talon"
Phone Number: 314-965-4853
Website: http://www.vianney.com
Alumni: Mark Lamping, president of the St. Louis Cardinals; Trent Green, NFL quarterback; Patrick Schuchard, artist; Bob Cassilly, sculptor and entrepreneur, founder of the City Museum

St. Joseph Academy

Date Founded: 1840
Location: 2307 South Lindbergh Boulevard, Frontenac
School Architecture: four-story, contemporary, brick building
School Namesake: St. Joseph
School History: St. Joseph Academy is a private, Catholic girls' high school. The Sisters of St. Joseph of Carondelet founded the school in a log cabin in 1836. In 1840, they opened the wing of a new building at 6400 Minnesota. In 1925, the school moved from the City's Carondelet neighborhood to Clayton, where it was located in one of the buildings on the Fontbonne College campus. In 1954, the number of students attending the Academy had grown, and the school moved to its present site.
Grades: 9-12
Current Enrollment: approximately 625 female students
Mascot: none, but sometimes referred to as the "Angels"
School Colors: green and white
School Motto: "Not I, But We"
School Paper: "Voice"
School Yearbook: "The Academy"
Distinguished Awards: Blue Ribbon School by the United States Department of Education
Phone Number: 314-965-7205
Website: www.stjosephacad.com
Alumni: Kristin Fokl, two-sport athlete (played on several women's professional basketball and volleyball teams)

St. Joseph High School

Date Founded: 1937
Location: 4132 Page Boulevard, St. Louis
School History: St. Joseph High School, run by the Sisters of St. Joseph, was founded in 1937 as the coeducational, Catholic, high school for blacks. It was originally located in the old Father Dunn

Newsboy Home, which was founded February 6, 1906, on Washington Avenue in St. Louis City and which became a home for "colored" boys on June 1, 1931, at 901 Garrison Avenue. A few years later, it moved to the St. Benedict Centre on West Belle, and then to the St. Ann Elementary School building at 4132 Page Boulevard and Whittier. It remained at St. Ann until it closed at the end of the 1950 – 1951 school year.
Grades: 9-12

St. Joseph's Home for Boys

Date Founded: 1846
Location: 4753 South Grand Avenue
School History: St. Joseph's Male Orphan Asylum was founded in 1846 in downtown St. Louis. In 1895, it moved to a building located at 4701 South Grand and became St. Joseph's Home for Boys. It remained there until it moved to 4753 South Grand Boulevard in 1935. The building is still in use.

St. Joseph Institute for the Deaf

Date Founded: 1837
Location: 1809 Clarkson Road, Chesterfield
School Namesake: named for the Sisters of St. Joseph who founded the school
School History: The Sisters of St. Joseph were established in the Carondelet area in 1836. At the request of Bishop Rosati, two of the sisters, Sister Celestine Pommerell and Sister St. John Founier, traveled to Lyons, France to learn sign language. They began teaching classes to deaf children in the Carondelet neighborhood in 1837. Through the years, they taught preschool- to eighth-grade classes for boys and girls in several locations, including 1483 82nd Boulevard in University City, until they moved to their next location in 1935. In 1997, St. Joseph Institute relocated to the new campus in Chesterfield. From this location, the staff teaches children from around the world using the latest technology, and today they have a 96% success rate of mainstreaming students into local high schools.
Current Enrollment: 77 students, preschool through eighth grade
Mascot: "Stingers"
School Colors: Cardinal red and Royal blue
School Paper: school publication
School Yearbook: pictures only, no words
Phone Number: 636-532-3211
Website: http://www.sjid.org

St. Louis Academy

Date Founded: August 2003
Location: 4601 Morganford, St. Louis City
School History: Dr. Jeff Benson founded the school in 2003 for emotionally and physically handicapped children between the ages of 6 and 18.
Grades: ages 6 to 18
Current Enrollment: 15 students
Phone Number: 314-481-5100
Website: http://www.saint louisacademy.org

St. Louis Christian Home

Date Founded: 1887
Location: 3033 North Euclid Avenue, St. Louis City
Phone Number: 314-381-3100

St. Louis Preparatory Seminary North

Date Founded: 1965
Location: 3500 St. Catherine in Florissant

School Namesake: named for the function and location
School History: St. Louis Preparatory Seminary North opened in 1965 for young men who were interested in becoming Catholic priests. The school was founded because of increasing enrollment. It began in the basement of Sacred Heart School building on North Jefferson in Florissant and moved to 3500 St. Catherine. In the spring of 1987, the school closed because of declining enrollment and was amalgamated with the St. Louis Preparatory Seminary South in Shrewsbury.
Grades: 9-12

St. Louis Preparatory Seminary South

Date Founded: 1957
Location: 5200 Shrewsbury Avenue in Shrewsbury
School Namesake: named for the function and location
School Site: grounds of Kenrick Seminary in Shrewsbury
School History: In 1957, a new high school facility was opened at 5200 Shrewsbury Avenue for young men who were interested in becoming Catholic priests. The new St. Louis Preparatory High School was located on the same grounds as Kenrick Seminary and the old St. Louis Preparatory High School that was founded in 1931. At that time, the "old Prep" became a four-year college known as "Cardinal Glennon College" and the "new Prep" became a four-year high school. The high school seminary closed in May 1991.
Grades: 9-12

Saint Louis Priory School

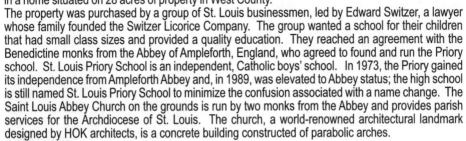

Date Founded: 1973
Location: 500 South Mason Road, West St. Louis County
Architect: Hellmuth Obata Kassabaum (HOK)
School Architecture: Contemporary, two-story, brick building
School Namesake: the religious organization that founded the school
School History: Saint Louis Priory school began in 1956 in a home situated on 28 acres of property in West County. The property was purchased by a group of St. Louis businessmen, led by Edward Switzer, a lawyer whose family founded the Switzer Licorice Company. The group wanted a school for their children that had small class sizes and provided a quality education. They reached an agreement with the Benedictine monks from the Abbey of Ampleforth, England, who agreed to found and run the Priory school. St. Louis Priory School is an independent, Catholic boys' school. In 1973, the Priory gained its independence from Ampleforth Abbey and, in 1989, was elevated to Abbey status; the high school is still named St. Louis Priory School to minimize the confusion associated with a name change. The Saint Louis Abbey Church on the grounds is run by two monks from the Abbey and provides parish services for the Archdiocese of St. Louis. The church, a world-renowned architectural landmark designed by HOK architects, is a concrete building constructed of parabolic arches.
Grades: 7 -12
Current Enrollment: approximately 390 students
Mascot: "Rebels"
School Colors: blue and red
School Paper: "Record"
School Yearbook: "The Shield"
Phone Number: 314-434-3690
Website: http://www.priory.org
Alumni: Kevin Kline, actor

St. Louis University High School (SLUH)

Date Founded: 1818
Location: 4970 Oakland Avenue (*see* school history, below)
School Architecture: three-story, ornate brick building with multiple towers that resembles an English castle
School Namesake: St. Louis
School History: In 1818, the Jesuits founded St. Louis Academy as a Catholic school for young men, charging tuition of $12 per quarter. It is the second oldest Jesuit high school in the United States. In 1832, it was chartered as "St. Louis University," and the high school was still called the Academy. Until 1924, the Jesuits staffed two high school campuses. One was St. Louis University High School on Grand and West Pine. The other was called "Loyola Hall St. Louis University High School," located on south Compton at Eads Avenue in the former James Buchanan Eads Mansion. As a result of a generous donation by Mrs. Anna Backer, a new school was built and the two high schools consolidated. In 1924, the school moved into the present location in central St. Louis City south of Forest Park. Since then, the school name has been "St. Louis University High School."
Grades: 9-12
Current Enrollment: 1,000 male students
Mascot: "Junior Billikens"
School Colors: blue and white
School Paper: "Prep News"
School Yearbook: "Dauphin" (traditional name for the eldest sons of the former kings of France)
Phone Number: 314-531-0330
Website: http://www.sluh.org
Alumni: Ed McCauley, NBA hall of fame; "Buzz" Westfall, the late St. Louis County Executive; Mel Price, U. S. congressman (D-IL); Tom Dooley, philanthropist, medical doctor and author; and Alfonso Cervantes, former St. Louis mayor

St. Mark the Evangelist High School

Date Founded: 1910
Location: 1327 Academy in St. Louis City
School History: St. Mark the Evangelist High School was founded in 1910 as a Catholic parish high school for girls. The Sisters of Dominican Congregation of Our Lady of the Rosary taught the students and managed the school. The school closed after the 1973 - 1974 school year.

St. Mary's High School

Date Founded: 1931
Location: 4701 South Grand Avenue
School Architecture: two-story, contemporary, brick building
Building Cost: $1,500,000
School Namesake: St. Mary
School History: St. Mary's High School was founded in 1931 as an Archdiocesan Catholic high school for boys. The first classes were conducted in some small wooden buildings on the grounds of St. Joseph's Home for Boys in south St. Louis. It originally was named "South Side High School." When the orphanage moved to a new site in 1935, St. Mary's moved into the orphanage's former building. In 1947, the name was changed to "St. Mary's High School;" and, in 1964, the present high school facility was built. In 1931, the Christian Brothers were put in charge, but they withdrew in 1933 when the Brothers of Mary, the Marianist Brothers, took over the management of the school.
Grades: 9-12

Current Enrollment: 505 students
Mascot: "Dragons"
School Colors: white and Green
School Paper: "Clarion"
Phone Number: 314-481-8400
Website: http://www.stmaryshs.com
Alumni: Francis Slay, St. Louis mayor

St. Mary's Orphan Home

Date Founded: 1900
Location: 5341 Emerson Avenue, in St. Louis City's Walnut Park neighborhood
Land Cost: $70, 000
School History: St. Mary's Orphan Home was built in 1900 on land that was part of the Wipperman estate, purchased with $70,000 from an anonymous donor. The orphanage's copper-domed bell tower became a neighborhood landmark. The orphanage closed in 1952 and was reopened as "St. Mary's Special School for Retarded Children." In addition, Laboure High School, a Catholic girls' high school, has shared the five-acre campus since 1942.

St. Mary's Special School for Exceptional Children

Date Founded: 1952
Location: 5341 Emerson Avenue, in St. Louis City's Walnut Park neighborhood
School Namesake: St. Mary
Site History: St. Mary's Orphan Home
School History: St. Mary's Special School for Retarded Children opened in 1952 at 5341 Emerson in the Walnut Park Neighborhood. It used the same building that was previously used by St. Mary's Orphan Home, built in 1900. The land, which was part of the Wipperman estate, was purchased with $70,000 from an anonymous donor. The orphanage's copper-domed bell tower became a neighborhood landmark. Laboure High School, a Catholic girls' high school, has shared the 5-acre campus since 1942. The students who attend St. Mary's are Catholic children with various types of physical and mental handicaps that prevent them from participating in regular school programs.
Grades: The school is for students 13-21 years of age.
Phone Number: 314-533-3454

St Peter High School (*see* Coyle High School)

St. Philomena Technical School

Date Founded: 1845
Location: 5300 Cabanne and Union, St. Louis's Cabanne neighborhood
School History: St. Philomena's Technical School for girls was founded at Fifth and Walnut in 1834 as an orphanage for poor girls. The orphanage was run by the by the Sisters of Charity of St. Vincent de Paul to protect child slaves, who were frequently overworked or physically abused. At the time, it was common practice for families to indenture or apprentice children at very young ages to make room for younger children. After 1845, St. Philomena's became a school for girls 14 and older. The younger girls were sent to St. Mary's Orphanage. In 1864, the school was located at Clark and Ewing Avenues. In 1910, it moved to a large brick building at the southwest corner of Union and Cabanne, in the Cabanne neighborhood. In the early days, the main source of income for the school was from the residents' sewing layettes, trousers, and fancy needlework. The school closed in 1960. The property is now used as a nursing home and Stella Maris day-care center.
Ages: 12-18 years

St. Stanislaus Seminary

Date Founded: 1823
Location: 700 Howdershell Road, Florissant
School Namesake: St. Stanislaus

School History: St. Stanislaus Seminary began in 1823, when eight Belgian Jesuit missionaries arrived in what is now known as Florissant and constructed a log building to serve as a their residence and as a school for Indians. In 1840, the seminarians replaced the original log structure with a Greek Revival facility made from limestone quarried from the cliffs overlooking the Missouri River, bricks made on site, and lumber from local forests. For more than 100 years, the self-sufficient seminary educated and trained new Jesuit priests. The seminary closed in 1971. The newer facilities were purchased by the Gateway College of Evangelism, which is still in operation. The original limestone structure, now known as the "Rock Museum Building," was turned into a museum of Jesuit history.
Phone Number: (museum) 314-837-3525

St. Theresa Academy

Date Founded: 1894
Location: 25th Street and Ridge Avenue in East St. Louis
School Architecture: contemporary, all-brick, two-story building
School Namesake: named for St. Thersea
School History: St. Theresa High School was a Catholic academy for girls run by the Sisters of the Precious Blood. The high school was located in Winstanley Park in East St. Louis, Illinois, directly across the Mississippi River from the City of St. Louis. When St. Theresa Academy closed in 1974, its students transferred to Assumption High School.
Mascot: none. Graduates had an unusual class ring inscribed with "STA" and an artist's palette-like symbol. The ring was worn on the little finger.
School Colors: red and white

St. Thomas Aquinas High School

Date Founded: 1957
Location: Florissant
School History: St. Thomas Aquinas High School was founded by the Sisters of St. Joseph at the request of Cardinal Ritter to establish a ninth-grade center in Florissant. In 1985, what had become St. Thomas Aquinas high school merged with Mercy High School, creating St. Thomas Aquinas-Mercy High School, which was located on 845 Dunn Road in Florissant.
Grades: 9-12
Mascot: "Falcons"
School Colors: blue and gold

St. Thomas Aquinas-Mercy High School

Date Founded: July 1, 1985
Location: 845 Dunn Road, Florissant
School History: St. Thomas Aquinas-Mercy High School was founded as an Archdiocesan, coeducational school on July 1, 1985, as a result of a merger between St. Thomas Aquinas High School and Mercy High School. The school closed at the end of the 2002-2003 school year. On August 21, 2003, Trinity Catholic High School opened at the site of Rosary High School on Redman Avenue. Trinity is the result of a merger between St. Thomas Aquinas-Mercy High School, on Dunn Road in Florissant, and Rosary High School, on 1720 Redman Road in Spanish Lake, the site of the new school.
Grades: 9-12
Enrollment: 2002-2003 enrollment was 324 students
Mascot: "Falcons"
School Colors: blue and gold
Website: http://www.aquinas-mercy.org

St. Vincent Home for Children

Date Founded: 1850
Location: 7401 Florissant Road, St. Louis County
School History: St. Vincent Home for Children was founded in 1850, following a cholera epidemic and fire. Both disasters occurred in 1849 and orphaned many St. Louis children. Because existing Catholic diocesan orphanages were full, an appeal was made to the German Catholic community. The appeal was successful, raising money for construction of a new orphanage in 1851. The Sisters of St. Joseph of Carondelet administered the home until 1888, when the Sisters of Christian Charity assumed the administration of the orphanage.
Phone Number: 314-261-6011

Tower Grove Christian School

Date Founded: 1978
Location: 14257 Magnolia Avenue, St. Louis City
School Architecture: contemporary
School Namesake: location
Site History: Tower Grove Baptist Church
School History: The school was founded in 1978 as a mission of the Tower Grove Baptist Church and is part of the church facility. It is a coeducational, Christian school.
Grades: kindergarten to 12th
Current Enrollment: approximately 95 high school students
Mascot: "Tiger"
School Colors: red and white
School Paper: none
School Yearbook: currently "Overcomer;" changes yearly
Phone Number: 314-776-6473
Website: http://www.tgcs.net/

Trinity Catholic High School

Date Founded: August 21, 2003
Location: 1720 Redman Road, Spanish Lake
School Architecture: two-story, contemporary, brick and glass building
School Namesake: Holy Trinity (students selected name by vote)
Site History: Rosary High School
School History: St. Thomas Aquinas-Mercy High School and Rosary High School closed in June of 2003, and the students began the 2003-2004 school year in a new school named "Trinity High School," an Archdiocesan Catholic, coeducational school. The building and property for Trinity were formerly Rosary High School, located in Spanish Lake and run by the School Sisters of Notre Dame.
Grades: 9-12
Current Enrollment: approximately 400 students
Mascot: "Titans"
School Colors: red, white and silver (voted on by students)
School Yearbook: "Trinity"
Phone Number: 314-741-1333
Website: http://www.trinitycatholichighschool.org/contact.hem

Ursuline Academy

Date Founded: 1848
Location: 341 Sappington Road, Kirkwood
School Architecture: three-story, brick traditional and
two-story, brick contemporary
School Namesake: named for the Ursuline Sisters who
founded the academy
School History: Ursuline Academy is a private, Catholic
girls' high school. Four Ursuline Sisters from Austria and
Bavaria founded Ursuline Academy in 1848 at the request

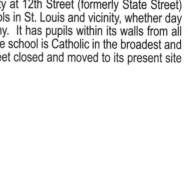

of Bishop Kenrick. The school was located in St. Louis City at 12th Street (formerly State Street)
between Ann and Russell Avenue. "None of the many schools in St. Louis and vicinity, whether day
or boarding schools, have a better record than this Academy. It has pupils within its walls from all
parts of the country, and of many different creeds, though the school is Catholic in the broadest and
best sense of the term."[1] In 1926, the academy on 12th Street closed and moved to its present site
in Kirkwood.
Grades: 9-12
Current Enrollment: 636 female students
Mascot: "Bear"
School Motto: SERIAM, "I will serve"
School Colors: red and white
School Paper: "Bear Facts"
School Yearbook: "Oak Leaves"
Phone Number: 314-966-4556
Website: http:// www.ursulinestl.org
Alumnae: Jane Mitchelette Hanneker (1948) businesswoman, recipient of "Woman of Achievement
Award" 2004

Villa Duchesne High School

Date Founded: 1929
Location: 801 South Spoede Road, West St. Louis
County
School Architecture: French Chateau style
School Namesake: Rose Philippine Duchesne (1769-
1852), a religious of the Society of the Sacred Heart
known as Mother Duchesne, founder and supervisor of
many schools. She was canonized a saint in the Roman
Catholic Church on July 4, 1988.

School History: The Religious of the Sacred Heart founded Villa Duchesne School in 1929. The
private, Catholic girls' school is located in west St. Louis County. In 1968, City House High School
closed, and the students transferred to Villa Duchesne.
Grades: K-6 boys and girls, 7-12 girls only
Current Enrollment: 400 female students between grades 7-12
Mascot: "Saints"
School Colors: maroon and white
School Paper: "Tower Talk"
School Yearbook: *Entree Nous* ("We Enter")
Distinguished Awards: Blue Ribbon School by the United States Department of Education
Phone Number: 314-432-2021
Website: http://www.vdoh.org/

---

[1]*Commercial and Architectural St. Louis Illustrated.* St. Louis: Jones & Orear, Publishers, 1888
[n.p.]

Visitation Academy

Date Founded: 1833
Location: 3020 North Ballas Road, West St. Louis County
Architect: McMahan, current building; Christner, 2000 addition
School Namesake: Sisters of the Visitation (The Visitation Mary by her cousin)
Site History: fields

School History: Visitation Academy ("Viz"). The Order of the Visitation was founded in Annecy, Haute Savoie, by St. Francis de Sales and Ste. Jan Frances de Chautal in 1610, and was introduced in the United States in 1799 at Georgetown, in Washington, D. C. The Sisters of the Visitation founded the first Academy of the Visitation in the Archdiocese of St. Louis in Kaskaskia, Illinois, in 1833. In April 1844, the Sisters opened their first school for girls in St. Louis City on Sixth Street. Increased enrollment and a gift of property in 1858 from Anne Mullanphy Biddle enabled the Sisters to build a large, three-story, boarding and day school on Cass Avenue between 19th and 21st Streets. "It was ranked for over a half a century among the best patronized educational institutions in the west."[2] In 1892, Visitation moved west to a large, French chateau-style building at the southeast corner of Cabanne and Belt Avenue. The building was designed by Barnett, Haynes and Barnett and served as the location for Visitation Academy until 1962, when the need for expanded modern facilities led the school to move to its present location. After the sisters departed, the original structure was torn down and St. Louis City purchased the 10-acre site. Visitation Park now stands on the site of the earlier high school, and remnants of the former gymnasium still remain.
Grades: Pre-kindergarten through high school
Current Enrollment: approximately 433 females
Mascot: none; per school vote, the teams are known as "Vivettes," which means "girl who lives Jesus"
School Colors: red and white
School Paper: "Viz-itor", past; "Paper Moon" (named for crescent jewelry given to graduates)
School Yearbook: "The Crescent"
Phone Number: 314-432-5353
Website: http://www.visitationacademy.org
Alumni: Wendy Wiese, St. Louis radio personality; Mary Engelbreit, artist and entrepreneur

Westminster Christian Academy

Date Founded: 1976
Location: 10900 Ladue Road in St. Louis County
Architect: Mitchell Hudgeback, Inc., designed the expansion of the former Ladue High School
School Architecture: two-story, brick, campus style
Building Cost: The land and building of the former Ladue Junior High School was purchased for $3,000,000 in 1982; modernization and expansion cost an additional $11,000,000.
School Namesake: Westminster Confession of Faith
Site History: Ladue Junior High School
School History: Westminster Christian Academy was founded in 1976 as an independent, coeducational, Christian school and was originally located at Missouri Baptist College. Later, Westminster moved into a facility in Kirkwood. In 1982, the Academy's board of directors purchased the former Ladue Junior High School Building at 10900 Ladue Road. In 2003, the Westminster

---

[2]*Commercial and Architectural St. Louis Illustrated.* St. Louis: Jones & Orear, Publishers, 1888 [n.p.]

school board purchased the former West County Technical High School at 13480 South Outer Forty Drive in Chesterfield.
Grades: 7 to 12
Current Enrollment: approximately 800 male and female students
Mascot: "Wildcat"
School Colors: Royal blue and white
School Paper: was "The Roar;" now "Ambassador"
School Yearbook: "Foundation"
Phone Number: 314-997-2900
Website: http://www.wcastl.com
Alumni: Jack Oliver, speechwriter

Xavier High School

Date Founded: 1934
Location: 3733 West Pine in St. Louis City
Site History: St. Louis University
School History: St. Xavier High School was founded in 1934 by the Sisters of Charity as a private Catholic high school for girls on the campus of St. Louis University. A new building was constructed in 1950. The high school closed at the end of the 1973 school year.

Independent High Schools

Annie Malone Children's Home

Date Founded: 1946
Location: 2612 Annie Malone Drive
School Architecture: two-story, brick colonial building, with cupolas on the top and tall columns at the main front entrance
School Namesake: named in honor of Annie Minerva Turnbo Pope Malone
Site History: Originally St. Louis Colored Orphan's Home
School History: In 1946, the St. Louis Colored Orphan's Home was renamed in honor of Annie Minerva Turnbo Pope Malone and is now known as the Annie Malone Children's Home. The home is supported by the United Way and by the Annie Malone May Day Parade, held annually on the last Sunday in May in The Ville neighborhood.
Phone Number: 314-531-0120

Chesterfield Day School

Date Founded: 1998
Location: 123 Schoolhouse Road, St. Albans
Architect: Mitchell Hudgeback
School Architecture: Sprawling country home
School Namesake: location where school was founded
Site History: Walnut Orchard
School History: Chesterfield Day School has two campuses. It began in 1962 as a school for toddlers through sixth grade, located at 1100 White Road in Chesterfield. In 1998, a second campus opened in St. Albans. The school began with seventh-grade students who attended class in a privately owned, 100-year-old, refurbished schoolhouse on Basset Road. When construction was completed in 1999, the school moved to its present location at 123 Schoolhouse Road and now serves toddlers through 12th grade at the St. Albans campus.
Grades: toddlers through 12th
Current Enrollment: approximately 22 coeducational high school students
Mascot: "Eagle"
School Colors: Navy blue and white
School Paper: name changes
School Yearbook: name changes yearly
Phone Number: 636-458-6688
Website: http://www.chesterfielddayschool.org

Crossroads School

Date Founded: 1974
Location: 500 DeBaliviere, St. Louis City
School Architecture: long, single-story, brick building
Site History: stores before the school
School History: Crossroads School was founded by Arthur and Carol Lieber as a privately operated school, beginning as an independent junior high school in St. Louis's Laclede Town. In 1976, the school moved to 4532 Lindell, and then later to 500 DeBaliviere. In 1985, Crossroads High School was accredited as a Junior and Senior High School.
Grades: 7-12
Current Enrollment: approximately 162 coeducational students in grades 9-12
Mascot: "Current", river current
School Colors: blue and white
School Paper: "Voice"
School Yearbook: "Crossroads"

Phone Number: 314-367-8085
Website: http://www.crossroads-school.org

John Burroughs School

Date Founded: 1923
Location: 755 South Price Road St. Louis County
Architect: LaBeaume and Klein
School Architecture: Spanish Mediterranean
School Namesake: John Burroughs, naturalist and actor
Site History: 17.5 acres of unused property near United
Railroad right of way
School History: John Burroughs School was founded
in 1923 by a group of parents who wanted to follow the
philosophy of John Dewey. The school was to be progressive, coeducational, non-sectarian,
and college preparatory. The founders believed, as students believe today, in the service ethic, in
simplicity, concern for nature, democracy, diversity, and the highest academic standards.
Grades: 9-12
Current Enrollment: approximately 600 female and male students
Mascot: none (teams called the "Bombers")
School Colors: blue and gold
School Paper: "World"
School Yearbook: "The Governor"
Phone Number: 314-993-4040
Website: http://jbworld.jbs.st-louis.mo.us/
Alumni: Edward ("Tad") Foote II, former University of Miami president; Kiku Obata, nationally
renowned graphic designer; John Hartford, Grammy Award-winning musician and composer

Logos School

Date Founded: September 14, 1970
Location: 9137 Old Bonhomme, St. Louis County
School Namesake: LOGOS means "word, speech or understanding" in Greek.
School History: Logos School opened with four students on September 14, 1970, in a warehouse
in the Central West End. Logos is a coeducational high school that is organized as a not-for-profit
educational corporation. In 1982, with 30 students, the school moved into the former Ladue
elementary school located on Bonhomme. The building was originally leased, then purchased, from
the Ladue School District. In 1991, seventh and eighth grades were added to the coeducational
school.
Grades: 7-12
Current Enrollment: approximately 140 students
Mascot: "Explorers"
School Colors: blue and gold
Phone Number: 636-997-7002
Website: http://www.logosschool.org

Mary Institute

Date Founded: May 11, 1859
Location: Lucas, Locust Avenue, and 455 Lake Avenue
in St. Louis City, 101 North Warson Road in St. Louis
County
School Architecture: Lake Avenue location was a two-
story, ornamental brick building that looks like an English
castle; the Warson Road location is a two-story, brick,
classical colonial style with four columns at the entrance
Building Cost: $25,000 (Lucas Place), $70,000 (Locust

Avenue)
School Namesake: Mary Eliot, daughter of William G. Eliot, co-founder of Mary Institute
School History: Mary Institute was established as a private, girls' high school in St. Louis in May 11, 1859. Its co-founder was William Greenleaf Eliot, the prominent Unitarian Minister who founded Washington University in 1853. It was the first non-sectarian school for girls in the U. S. The school was named for his daughter, who died at the age of 17. It opened on the day she would have celebrated her 21st birthday. Its first site was on Lucas Place; in 1878, it relocated to Locust Avenue and Beaumont (22nd Street). In 1901, the school moved again to a new building on Lake Avenue. The school remained at that location until 1928, when an alumna donated 22 acres, and Washington University added 18 more acres for the new high school on Warson Road in St. Louis County. In 1972, New City School purchased the former Mary Institute building at 455 Lake Avenue between Waterman and Westminster. New City School opened in 1969, and the classrooms were leased from the First Unitarian Church at Kingshighway and Waterman for (ages 3-4 years to 6th grade). MICDS (*see below*) opened in 1993, when a full-scale alliance created a single school from Mary Institute and St. Louis Country Day School
Alumni: Betty Grable (attendee), actress; Sara Teasdale, Pulitzer prize-winning poet; Mrs. Horton Watkins, philanthropist

Mary Institute Country Day High School (MICDS)

Date Founded: 1993
Location: 101 North Warson Road, St. Louis County
School Architecture: two-story, brick, classical colonial style with four columns at the entrance
School Namesake: named for Mary Institute and Country Day School
Site History: formerly Mary Institute and St. Louis Country Day School
School History: Mary Institute Country Day School (MICDS) formally opened in 1993, when a full-scale alliance created a single school from Mary Institute and Country Day School. The new school has one board and a common administration, faculty, student body and curriculum. The coeducational school serves students from junior kindergarten through grade 12.
Grades: Pre-K- 12
Current Enrollment: 580 (grades 9-12)
Mascot: "Ram"
School Colors: red and green
School Paper: "Voice"
School Yearbook: "Phoenix"
Phone Number: 314-995-7367
Website: http://www.micds.org

Missouri School for the Blind

Date Founded: 1851
Location: 3815 Magnolia Avenue, St. Louis City
School History: The Missouri School for the Blind was established in 1851 by Eli William Whalen. Mr. Whalen was a blind man who had formerly been Superintendent of the Tennessee Institution for the Blind at Nashville. The school was the first in the western hemisphere to teach the reading and writing of Braille.
Current Enrollment: 22 in 2002
Phone Number: 314-776-4320
Website: http://www.msb.k12.mo.us

Poro College

Date Founded: 1917
Location: Corner of St. Ferdinand and Billips Avenues, in The Ville neighborhood
School Architecture: three-story, pie-shaped, brick building
School Namesake: named for Poro, a hair product
School History: Poro College was founded 1917 by Annie Minerva Turnbo Pope Malone and was located at the corner of St. Ferdinand and Billips Avenues in The Ville neighborhood. Poro College was neither a college nor a vocational high school in the traditional sense. It was a private company that trained blacks as beauticians and sales people from around the country for Poro products. Poro was a trademarked brand of scalp treatment developed by Annie Malone for growing and straightening hair. After she moved her company from Peoria to St. Louis in 1902, it provided approximately 200 jobs for Ville residents. In addition, Poro College functioned as a community center; in 1927, after a disastrous tornado struck St. Louis, the College served as a Red Cross relief center. Annie Malone was America's first African-American female millionaire and one of Missouri's first self-made millionaires. In 1930, Annie moved her company to Chicago to expand her business, and the Poro College building was used as a hotel. In 1939, the building became Lincoln University Law School, Missouri's first African-American university law program. In 1965, St. James Methodist Episcopal Church purchased the building and demolished it to make room for a senior-citizen apartment complex known as the "James House." In 1946, the St. Louis Colored Orphans' Home was renamed in honor of Annie Minerva Turnbo Pope Malone, and is now known as the Annie Malone Children's Home. The home is supported by the United Way and by the Annie Malone May Day Parade, held annually on the last Sunday in May in The Ville neighborhood.
Grades: various ages

St. Louis Country Day School

Date Founded: September 29, 1917
Location: Kingshighway and Maryland, in St. Louis City; Brown Road and 101 North Warson Road, in St. Louis County
School Architecture: two-story, brick, classical colonial style with four columns at the entrance
School History: St. Louis Country Day School opened on September 29, 1917, with 45 male students. The high school was located in St. Louis at Kingshighway and Maryland. In 1925, a new facility was built, and the school moved into St. Louis County on Brown Road until 1958, when it moved to its present location on North Warson Road in St. Louis County. In 1993, the school formed an alliance with Mary Institute to create Mary Institute Country Day School (MICDS).
Alumni: Vincent Price, actor; U. S. Senators John Danforth (R-MO) and Thomas Eagleton (D-MO); and Pete Wilson, former governor of California

Smith Academy and Manual Training School

Date Founded: 1905
Location: 5351 Enright Avenue, in St. Louis City's Cabanne Neighborhood
Architect: Mauran, Russell and Garden
School Architecture: restrained Classical Revival, red brick, terra cotta and stone
Building Cost: $275,000
School History: Smith Academy and Manual Training School was built in 1905 as a private school for boys, sponsored by Washington University for elite clientele. It was located on Enright Avenue in the Cabanne area. It closed in 1916. After a tragic fire at Christian Brothers College High School, the students attended school in the closed Smith Academy on Cabanne, which was loaned to them by Washington University. In 1917, Washington University sold the facility to the St. Louis Board of Education. In 1918, the St. Louis Board of Education opened it as the "Ben Blewett Junior High School." In 1931, it became a four-year high school called "Ben Blewett High School." In 1948, the

high school closed and Harris Teachers College moved into the building from 1517 South Teresa. The college remained in the building until 1963, when it moved to the former location of Vashon High School at 3026 Laclede. In 1963, the building became Enright Middle School for sixth and seventh grades; and, in 1975, it became Enright Ninth Grade Center as a supplement to Soldan High School.
Grades: 9-12
School Colors: red and white
Alumni: T. S. Elliot, poet; St. Louis mayors Henry W. Kiel (1913-1925) and William Dee Becker (1941-1943)

The Churchill School

Date Founded: 1978
Location: 1035 Price Road, St. Louis County
School Namesake: Sir Winston Churchill
School History: The Churchill School is a private, coeducational school for children with learning disabilities. It began in the old Maryland School as a summer-session program in 1978 and became a full-time school in 1980. It moved to its present location in August 1984. The school is named in honor of Sir Winston Churchill, who successfully overcame his learning disabilities. Its goal is to educate children with learning disabilities so that they can later be mainstreamed into traditional classrooms.
Grades: 2nd to 10th
Current Enrollment: 120 students for all grades
Mascot: "Bulldog"
School Colors: green and white
School Paper: "Winston Weekly"
School Yearbook: "Victory Magazine"
Phone Number: 314-997-4343
Website: http://www.churchillschool.org
Alumni: Rodney Hamilton, Juilliard School graduate and well-known dancer

Thomas Jefferson School

Date Founded: 1946
Location: 4100 South Lindbergh Boulevard, St. Louis County
School Namesake: Thomas Jefferson, President of the U. S. (1801-1809)
School History: Robin McCoy, Charles E. Merrill, Jr. and Graham Hill founded Thomas Jefferson School as a private boarding school in 1946. For the first 25 years, the school provided a 9th –12th grade education to approximately 40 boys each year. In 1971, the school became coeducational; in a few years, the girl-to-boy ratio reached approximately 50:50. During the 1970s, the school also began admitting students as five-day boarders. The school is located on 20 acres in south St. Louis County.
Grades: 7-12
Current Enrollment: approximately 75 students
Mascot: "Titans"
School Colors: Royal blue and white
School Paper: "Declaration"
School Yearbook: changes yearly
Phone Number: 314-843-4151
Website: http://www.tjs.org

Whitfield School

Date Founded: 1952
Location: 175 S. Mason Road in Town and Country
Architect: Mitchell Hudgeback
School Architecture: single-story, brick, contemporary
School Namesake: small tutorial school in England
Site History: school began in a private home with 20 students
School History: John Barnes and Allen Cole founded Whitfield School as a tutorial school in 1952 and as an entrepreneurial operation with a minimal capital investment. For many years, the school functioned as a for-profit business, and the building now known as the Barnes and Cole Alumni House served both as the school building and as the founders' residence. In 1970, the school became non-profit.
Grades: 6-12
Current Enrollment: approximately 280 male and female students in grades 9-12
Mascot: "Warrior" (gladiator type)
School Colors: green and white
School Paper: "Odyssey"
School Yearbook: "Iliad"
Phone Number: 314-434-5141
Website: http://today.whitfieldschool.org

Wyman Hall High School

Date Founded: Chartered on February 27, 1851
Location: Market Street near the Courthouse
School Namesake: founder Edward Wyman
School History: Wyman Hall School was the first private high school to be incorporated in St. Louis; it was chartered on February 27, 1851. Mr. Edward Wyman founded the all-boys' school. In earlier times, Mr. Wyman was involved in a number of schools, dating back to 1843. He began his first school, English and Classical High School, with a single student; the rent was $8.00 per month. In 1852, his high school enrollment grew to 300 boys; but, in 1853, he lost some of his students when they transferred to the new public high school.

Maps

St. Louis des Illinois 1780 Village
160

St. Louis, Missouri 1822
161

St. Louis's First Public High Schools
162

St. Louis City Parochial High Schools
164

St. Louis Public High Schools
166

St. Louis Area School Districts
168

St. Louis des Illinois 1780

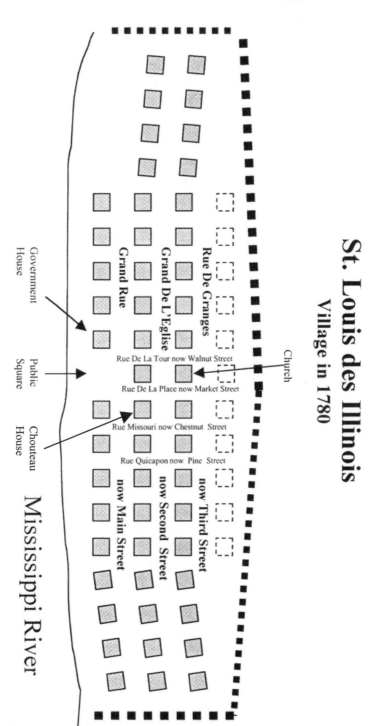

St. Louis, Missouri 1822

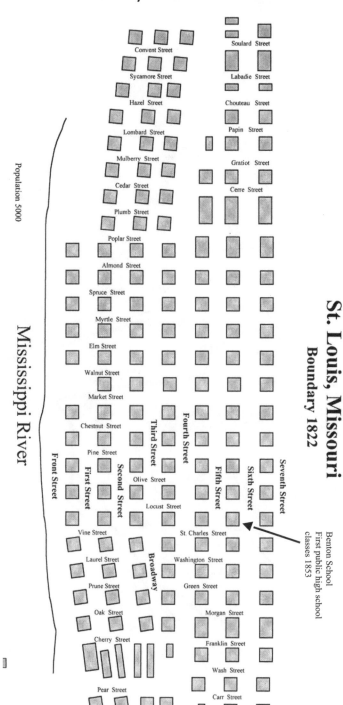

Population 5000

Mississippi River

St. Louis, Missouri
Boundary 1822

Benton School
First public high school
classes 1853

St. Louis's First Public High Schools

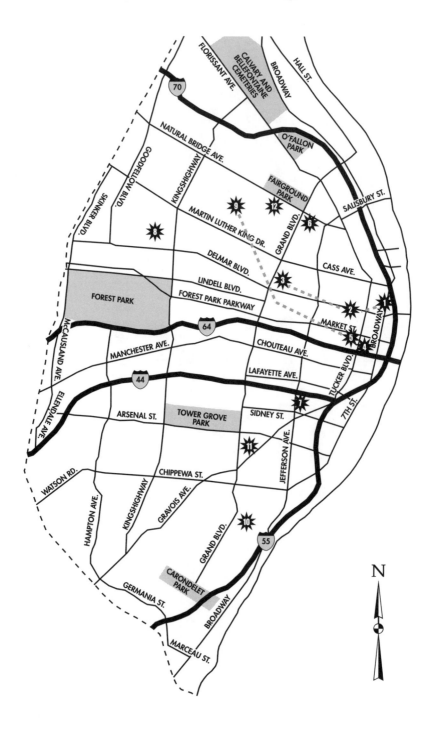

St. Louis's First Public High Schools

1. **First Public High School**
   6th & St. Charles
   Benton School
   1853-1856

2. **High School**
   15th & Olive
   1856-1893

3. **Central High School**
   1030 N. Grand
   1893-1927

4. **Sumner High School**
   11th & Spruce Streets
   1875-1897

5. **Sumner High School**
   15th & Walnut Streets
   1897-1910

6. **Yeatman High School** 1904-1927
   Central High School 1927-1984
   3616 Garrison

7. **McKinley High School**
   3156 Russell
   1904-1989

8. **Soldan High School**
   918 N. Union Blvd.
   1909-Present

9. **Sumner High School**
   4248 W. Cottage Ave.
   1910-Present

10. **Cleveland High School**
    4352 Louisiana
    1915-Present

11. **Roosevelt High School**
    3220 Hartford St.
    1925-Present

12. **Beaumont High School**
    3836 Natural Bridge Rd.
    1926-Present

St. Louis City Parochial High Schools

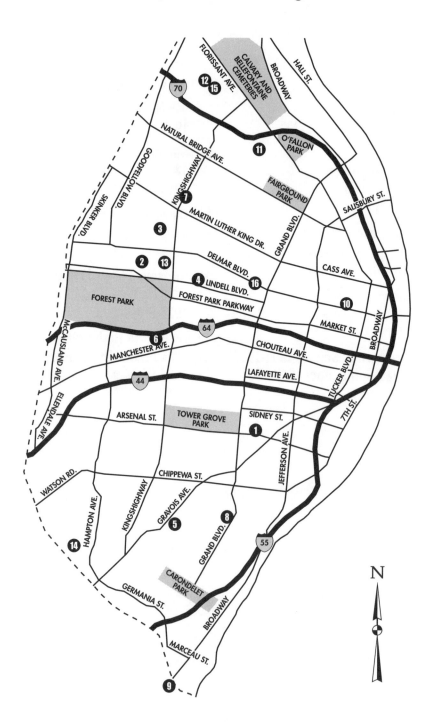

St. Louis City Parochial High Schools

1. **St. Elizabeth Academy**
   3401 Arsenal
   1882-Present

2. **Visitation Academy**
   Cabanne & Belt
   Founded 1833
   1892-1962 at this location

3. **The Principia Upper School**
   Page & Belt Avenues
   1910-1961

4. **Rosati-Kain High School**
   4389 Lindell
   1912-Present

5. **St. John the Baptist**
   5021 Atkins
   1922-Present

6. **St. Louis University High School**
   4970 Oakland
   Founded 1818
   1924-Present at current location

7. **McBride Catholic High School**
   1909 N. Kingshighway
   1925-1971

8. **St. Mary High School**
   4701 S. Grand Ave.
   1931-Present

9. **Notre Dame High School**
   320 E. Ripa Ave.
   1934-Present

10. **St. Joseph (Blacks) High School**
    Washington Ave.
    1937

11. **DeAndreis Catholic High School**
    4275 Clarence
    1942-1976

12. **Laboure Catholic High School**
    5421 Thekla
    1942-1979

13. **Lutheran High School**
    Lake & Waterman Avenues
    1946-1965

14. **Bishop DuBourg High School**
    5850 Eichelberger
    1950-Present

15. **Cardinal Ritter High School**
    5421 Thekla
    1979-2002

16. **Cardinal Ritter High School**
    701 N. Spring
    2002-Present

St. Louis Public High Schools

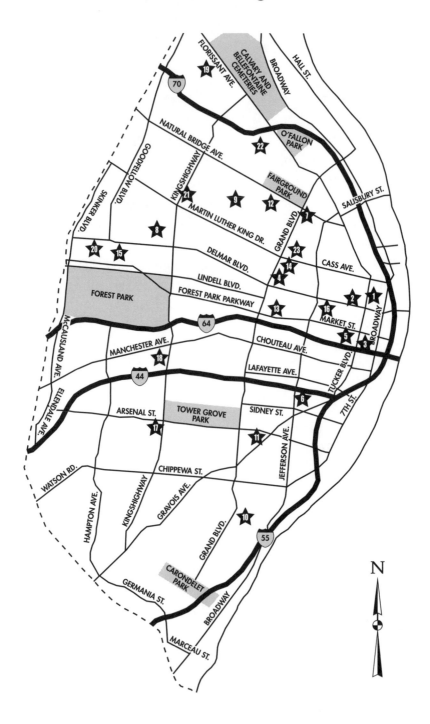

St. Louis Public High Schools

1. **First Public High School**
   6th & St. Charles
   Benton School
   1853-1856
2. **High School**
   15th & Olive
   1856-1893
3. **Charles Sumner High School**
   11th & Spruce
   1875-1897
4. **Central High School** 1893-1927
   Clyde C. Miller Career Academy
   Opened 2004
   1030 N. Grand, 1000 N. Grand
5. **Charles Sumner High School**
   15th & Walnut
   1897-1910
6. **William McKinley High School**
   Mass Media Program
   2156 Russell
   1904-1988
7. **Yeatman High School** 1904-1927
   Central High School 1927-1984
   Central Visual & Performing Arts
   1984-2004
   3616 Garrison
8. **Frank Louis Soldan H.S.** 1909-1948
   Soldan-Blewett H.S. 1948-1955
   Soldan High School 1955-1990
   Sr. Classical Academy 1981-1990
   Soldan International Studies 1993-
   Present
   918 N. Union Blvd.
9. **Charles Sumner High School**
   4248 W. Cottage
   1910-Present
10. **Grover Cleveland H.S.** 1915-1984
    Cleveland NJROTC 1984-Present
    4352 Louisiana
11. **Theodore Roosevelt H.S.** 1925-Present
    **Academy of Language &
    International Studies** 1985-1993
    Sr. Classical Academy 1990-1992
    3230 Hartford St.

12. **William Beaumont High School**
    3836 Natural Bridge
    1926-Present
13. **George B. & John B. Vashon H.S.**
    3026 Laclede
    1927-1963
14. **Herbert H. Hadley Vocational** 1927-1963
    Vashon High School 1963-2002
    3405 Bell
15. **Ben Blewett High School**
    5351 Enright
    1933-1948
16. **B.T. Washington Vocational H.S.**
    1934-1956
    Business, Management 1980-1986
    **Center for Management, Law and
    Public Policy** 1896-1993
    Continued Education 1993-1995
    814 N. 19th St.
17. **Southwest High School** 1937-1993
    Roosevelt at Southwest 1994-1995
    Central Visual & Performing Arts
    Present
    3125 S. Kingshighway
18. **O'Fallon Technical** 1956-1992
    Visual & Performing Arts 1976-1978
    Gateway Institute of Technology
    1992-Present
    5101 McRee
19. **Northwest High School**
    5140 Riverview
    1964-1992
20. **Delmar High School**
    5883 Delmar
    1975-1980
21. **Martin Luther King H.S.** 1975-1980
    Tri-A Outreach Center 1993-2003
    1909 N. Kingshighway
22. **Academy of Math & Science**
    4275 Clarence
    1976-1992
23. **George B. & John B. Vashon H. S.**
    3035 Cass
    2002-Present

St. Louis Area School Districts

St. Louis Area School Districts

Affton
 Affton High (1930)
 W.F. Gaunt High School (1936)
Bayless
 Bayless Sr. High (1935)
Brentwood
 Brentwood High (1927)
Clayton
 Clayton High (1917)
Ferguson Florissant
 Central School (1894)
 Ferguson High School (1926)
 Berkeley High School (1937)
 McCluer High School (1957)
 McCluer North High (1971)
 Kinloch High School (1937 white)
 Kinloch High School (1937 black)
 John M. Vogt High School (1930)
 McCluer South Berkeley H.S. (2003)
Hancock
 Hancock High School (1919)
 Hancock Sr. High (1934)
Hazelwood
 Hazelwood High School (mid-1950s)
 Hazelwood Central High School (1976)
 Hazelwood East High School (1976)
 Hazelwood West High School (1975)
Jennings
 Jennings High School (1915)
 Fairview High School (1926)
Kirkwood
 Kirkwood High School (1866)
 Kirkwood Sr. High (1955)
Ladue
 Ladue Horton Watkins H.S. (1952)
Lindbergh
 Lindbergh Sr. High School (1950)
Maplewood-Richmond Heights
 Maplewood High School (1930)
 Maplewood-Richmond Heights High (1951)

Mehlville
 Oakville Sr. High (1974)
 Melhville Sr. High (1925, 1939, 1955)
Normandy
 Washington High School (1907)
 Normandy High School (1923)
 Normandy Technical School
Parkway
 Parkway Jr./Sr. High School (1957)
 Parkway Sr. High School (1961)
 Parkway Central High (1968)
 Parkway West High (1968)
 Parkway North High (1971)
 Parkway South High (1976)
 Fern Ridge High (1992)
Pattonville
 Pattonville High School (1935)
 Pattonville Sr. High (1971)
Ritenour
 Ritenour High School (1911)
 Ritenour High School (1950)
Riverview
 Riverview Gardens High School (1927)
 Riverview Gardens Sr. High(1957)
Rockwood
 Eureka High School (1909)
 Eureka Sr. High (1973)
 Lafayette High School (1960)
 Lafayette Sr. High School (1989)
 Marquette Sr. High School (1993)
 Rockwood Summit Sr. High (1994)
University City
 University City Sr. High (1930)
Valley Park
 Valley Park High School (1932)
 Valley Park Sr. High
Webster
 Webster Groves High (1889)
 Douglass High School (1925-1954)
Wellston
 Wellston High School (1923)
 Milliard Haulter High School (1962)
 Melvin Ray Eskridge High School (1979)

Sources:

Dr. Henry E. Anderson - Wellston School District
Fr. John Arnold, S.J. - President, DeSmet Jesuit High School
Eileen Banden – McCluer High School
Frances Beezley - Beaumont High School
Nancy Beaver - Riverview Gardens High School
Dr. Jeff Benson - St. Louis Academy
Bob Berndt - Hancock Place School District
Maggie Barry – McCluer North High School
Chuck Bolinger - Hazelwood School District
Mary P. Braun - St. Louis County Technical High Schools
Earl Brown - Brentwood School District
Sr. Lorraine Brueggeman – St. Elizabeth Academy
Mary Carriere Bruns – Southwest High School
Sr. Joyce Buckler - St. Joseph School for the Deaf
Dave Buzzel - St. Charles High School
Angela Calloni - Bishop DuBourg High School
Scott Carriere – Southwest High School
Pete Cerone – St. John Vianney High School
Byron Clemens - Gateway Technical High School
Alicia Collins, Principal – Hiram Neuwoehner School
Susan Corrington – Edgewood Children's Home
Paul Crisler - Principal, Lutheran North High School
Susan Keeley Cross – St. Theresa Academy
Tom Cygen – Assumption High School
Laura Davidson – Ladue School District
Barbara Decker - Lindbergh School District
Ernie Demba – Parkway High School (the first Parkway High School,
now Parkway Central High School)
Marsha Rosenberg Demba - University City High School
Tom Dickman – St. Louis University High School
Dan Dillon
Daniel Ehlenbeck – Assistant Superintendent Tech Education (Retired)
Pamela Fournier - Cleveland High School
Dr. Barbara Fulton – Chesterfield Day School
Sapna Galloway - Notre Dame High School
Cindy Gibson – Ritenour High School
Tom Gosebrink – Northwest High School
Arlene Grant – Gallaudet School
Judy Gustafson - Valley Park High School
Katie Harrison - Ritenour High School

Bill Heidger – St. Mary's High School & other Catholic High Schools
Thelma Hurtnet - Ursuline Academy
Nancy Ide - Special School District
Pat Kadlec – Ferguson - Florissant Archives
Miriam Kerns - Pattonville School District
Joanne Dill Kimerle - Cleveland High School
Richard Kimerle - Southwest High School
Diane King – St. Charles High School
Judie Koettker - St. John the Baptist
Dee Lawrence - Affton Sr. High School
Doug Leach - O'Fallon Technical High School & Hadley Technical High School
Ann May Leonard – St. Thomas Aquinas High School
Tim Leonard – St. Thomas Aquinas High School
Tara Little – Evangelical Children's Home
Sr. Mary Grace McCormack - Visitation Academy
Doris McPherson – Tower Grove Christian School
Marilyn Montibeller – Southview School
Jennifer Munford – Central Visual and Performing Arts High School
Gary Muther – John Burroughs School
Debbie Dykes O'Brien – Duchesne High School
Jackie William Overkamp - Jennings High School
Jane Pesek - Thomas Jefferson School
Marty Peters - Westminster Christian Academy
Pauletta Reed - Nerinx Hall High School
Larry Reid – Assumption High School
St. Louis Public Library
St. Louis County Public Library
Linda Ciolek Schmerber - Jennings School District
Ishmael Sistrunk - Normandy School District
Rob Staggenborg, APR - Christian Brothers College High School
Diana Stewart - Parkway School District
Rita Stewart – Eureka High School
Ellen Thomasson – Missouri Historical Society
Cathy Vespereny - Webster Groves School District
Sally Wear - Bayless
Dorothy Walker – Soldan High School
Natasha Webster – Maplewood-Richmond Heights School District
Ed White & Becky Marshall - Whitfield School
Sr. Karl Mary Winkelmann – St. Thomas Aquinas, Rosary and Trinity High Schools
Tom Wojciechowski – Chaminade College Preparatory School
Anne Woodhouse – Missouri Historical Society

Bibliography

Academic American Encyclopedia. Danbury, CT: Grolier Incorporated, 1989

A Century of Achievement In the St. Louis Public High Schools, 1853-1953. The Saint Louis Public School Journal, Research and Survey Series No. 11, 6:2, Feb. 1953

Amsler, Kevin. *Final Resting Place.* St. Louis: Virginia Publishing Company, 1997

Bartley, Mary. *St. Louis Lost.* St. Louis: Virginia Publishing Company, 1994

Browne, Gordon M. *St. Louis Country Day School – First 50 Years.*

Bruce, Tracy A. *Reflections: a History of the Mehlville School District and Its Communities.* The Donning Company, Publishers, 2002

Burnett, Betty. *St. Louis at War.* The Patrice Press, 1987: 21

City of St. Louis official Website. *History of St. Louis Neighborhoods.* http://stlouis.missouri.org/neighborhoods/history

Commercial and Architectural St. Louis Illustrated. St. Louis: Jones & Orear, Publishers, 1888

Corbett, Katherine T. *In Her Place: A Guide to St Louis Women's History.* St. Louis: Missouri Historical Society Press, 1999

"Cramped but Charming," St. Louis *Post-Dispatch,* 25 August 2003, n.p.

"Developers Offer Salvation to 1878 Mummary," St. Louis *Post-Dispatch,* 24 August 2003, n.p.

"Dream Becomes a Reality for New Cardinal Ritter Prep," St. Louis *Post-Dispatch,* 24 August 2003, n.p.

East St. Louis Action Research Project, http://www.eslarp.uiuc.edu/, "History of East St. Louis," http://www.eslarp.uiuc.edu/ibex/archive/default.htm

Faherty, S.J., William Barnaby. *The St. Louis Irish.* St. Louis: Missouri Historical Society Press, 2001

Ferguson: A City Remembered Pictorial History. St. Louis: Ferguson Historical Society, 1994

Flame and Steel: 1965-1966. St. Louis: John O'Fallon Technical High School, 1966

Fox, Elana V. *Inside the World's Fair of 1904: 1,* St. Louis: Elana V. Fox, 2003

Fox, Tim, ed. *Where We Live: A Guide to St. Louis Communities.* St. Louis: Missouri Historical Society Press, 1955

Hannon, Robert E., ed. and compiler. *St. Louis: Its Neighborhoods and Neighbors, Landmarks and Milestones.* St. Louis: St. Louis Regional Commerce and Growth Association, 1986

Huffman, Sharon A. *Enrollment Statistics, St. Louis Public Schools,* July 2004

Huffman, Sharon A. *Historical Listings of St. Louis Public High Schools,* Revised August 2004

Huffman, Sharon A. *Historical Listings of St. Louis Public Schools, Architects and Building Commissioners,* 2004

Huffman, Sharon A. *St. Louis Public Schools: 160 years of Challenge, Change and Commitment to the Children of St. Louis Public Schools,* 1999

Kinloch Yesterday, Today and Tomorrow. St. Louis: Kinloch History Committee,1983

Magnan, William B. and Marcella C. Magnan. *The Streets of St. Louis.* St. Louis: Virginia Publishing Company, 1996

McNulty, Elizabeth. *St. Louis Then and Now.* San Diego: Thunder Bay Press, 2000

Missouri Department of Elementary and Secondary Education. *Missouri School Directory 2001-2002.* Jefferson City: Missouri Department of Elementary and Secondary Education, published 2002

Newcomer, Audrey, Director of Archives. *Archdiocese of St. Louis, Historical Listings of Archdiocese of St. Louis Catholic High Schools*

North Webster, foreword by Julius K. Hunter. - Ann Morris and Henrietta Ambrose. Bloomington: Indiana University Press, 1933

Phillips, Claude A. *A History of Education in Missouri.* Jefferson City: Hugh Stephens Printing Company, 1911

Prim, James Neal. *Lion of the Valley: St. Louis, Missouri.* Pruett Publishing Company, 1981

Rothensteiner, Rev. John. *History of the Archdiocese of St. Louis in Its Various Stages of Development for A. D. 1673 to A. D. 1928, Volume II.* Wielandy, CO: Press of Blackwell, 1928

Schertel, Vernon G. *Historic Lemay 1700-1945*

School District of the City of St. Charles Sesquicentennial, February 14, 1846 – February 14, 1996

Smith, Irene Sanford. *Ferguson: a City and Its People.* Ferguson Historical Society, 1976

Stadler, Francis Hurd. *St. Louis Day by Day.* The Patrice Press, 1989

Start, Clarissa. *Webster Groves.* City of Webster Groves, 1975

Terry, Dickson. *Clayton: a History.* Von Hoffman Press, Inc., 1976

Theising, Andrew J. *East St. Louis: Made in USA*, St. Louis: Virginia Publishing Company, 2003

The Red Book 2002-2003 Archdiocese of St. Louis Catholic Secondary Education (Web- based publication) – http://www.archstl.org/ education/secondary

Toft, Carolyn Hewes with Lynn Josse. *St. Louis: Landmarks and Historic Districts.* St. Louis: Landmarks Association of St. Louis, Inc., 2002

Troen, Selwyn K. *The Public and the Schools, Shaping the St. Louis System 1838-1920.* Columbia: University of Missouri Press, 1975

Wallace, Caverly Scott. *Ballwin, the City with a Future,* 1979

Wells, Amy Stuart and Robert L. Crain. *Stepping Over the Color Line.* New Haven: Yale University Press, 1997

Wright, John A., Sr. *Kinloch: Missouri's First Black City.* New Haven: Arcadia Publishing, 2000

Where We Go To School. St. Louis: Missouri Historical Society, August 1995

"William B. Ittner Architect's Buildings Stand for His Vision of Education," St. Louis *Post-Dispatch,* 30 November 2003, n.p.

Wunnenberg's Metro-West St. Louis City and County Street Guide. St. Louis: St. Louis Area Maps, Inc., 2000

Index

Academy of Language and International Studies High School, 75
Academy of Mathematics and Science High School, 75
Academy of the Sacred Heart (City House), 10, **123**
Ackerman School, 75
Affton High School, **75-76**, 120
Alvarez and Marsal, 72
Annie Malone Children's Home, 153
Assumption High School, 123-124
Augustinian Academy for Boys, 33, **124**

Booker T. Washington Technical High School, **79**, 84
Barat Hall for Boys, 19, **124**, 128, 129
Barnett, Haynes and Barnett, **24-25**, 151
Bayless Senior High, 24, 40, **76**, 169
Beaumont High School, 24, 31, **77**, 106, 163, 167, 170
Benson, Sally Smith, 17
Benton School, 8, **77**, 80, 163, 167
Berkeley High, 42, 72, **78**, 94, 100, 169
Bishop DuBourg High School, 26, 33, 123, **124-125**, 165
Blewett High School, 18, 27, 32, 78-79, 113, 156, 167
Block Yeshiva High School, 53, **125**
Blow Branch High School, 32
Blow, Susan Elizabeth, 9
Bonsack and Pierce, 25, 90
Boulicult, Marcel, 25, 76
Brentwood High School, 41, **79**, 169
Bridge at Wirtz School, 79
Bridges Program, **69**, 79
Bridgeton Academy, 7
Brown *vs.* Board of Education, 36, 60
Burroughs (*see* John Burroughs School)
Business, Management and Finance Centers and Office High School, 80

Cardinal Ritter College Preparatory High School, 33, 72, **125-126**, 165

Career Education Academy, 80
Carmelite Monastery, 70, **126**
Center for Management, Law and Public Policy Education, 80
Central High School (1856), 12, 14, 17, 23, 27, **80-81**, 82, 84, 90, 99, 122, 163, 167
Central High School (Ferguson), 82
Central Institute for the Deaf, 80
Central Visual and Performing Arts High School, 18, **82**, 87, 99, 101, 116, 122, 167
Cerre, Marie Therese, 6
Chaminade College Prep, 19, 27, 52, **126-127**
Chesterfield Day School, 153-154
Cholera, 66
Chouteau, Auguste, 5-6
Christian Academy of Greater St. Louis, 127
Christian Brothers College High School, 10, 18, 52, 72, **127-128**, 129, 156
Christian Orphans Home, 128
Christner Partnership, 151
Churchill School (*see* The Churchill School)
City House, 10, 14, 25, 123, 124, **128-129**, 150
Civil War, **11-14**, 58
Clayton High School, 26, 41, **82-83**, 169
Cleveland High School, 19, 23, **83**, 84, 110, 163
Cleveland Junior Naval Academy High School, 83-84
Clinton Branch High School, 12
Clyde C. Miller Career Academy, 64, 72, 80, **84**, 119, 120, 167
Colored Vocational High School, 84
Community Access Job Training, 85
Computers in schools, 73
Concordia Seminary, 70, **129**
Constitutional Amendments, 58
Continued Education High School Program (*see also* Meda P. Washington High School Program), 85
Cor Jesu High School, 52, **129**
Corpus Christi High School, 129-130
Cote Brilliante Branch High School, 23, 32
Country Day, 17, 19, 53, 155, **156**
Coyle High School, 52, **130**, 143, 147
Crossroads School, 32, 53, **153-154**

DeAndreis Catholic High School, 33, 75, 125, 126, **130**, 138, 165
Delmar High School, 85
DeSmet Jesuit High School, 28, 52, **130**
Des Peres School, 9
Douglas High School, 12, 14
Douglas Branch High School, 12, 14
Douglass, Frederick, 85
Douglass High School, 50, 60, **85-86**, 94, 169
Drucker, Robert G., 125
DuBourg High School (*see* Bishop DuBourg H.S.)
Duchesne High School, 131

Eames and Young, 22
East St. Louis Senior High School, 86
Eden Seminary, 70, 104, **131**
Edgewood Children's Center, 68, **131-132**
Eliot Grammar School, 23, 116
English and Classical High School, 158
Enright Middle School, 18, **78-79,** 157
Epworth Children and Family Services, 68, **132**
Eskridge High School (*see* Melvin Ray Eskridge H.S.)
Eureka High School, 49, **86**, 96, 169
Eureka Senior High, 49, **86**
Evangelical Children's Home, 68, **132**

Fairview High School, 44, **86-87**, 93, 169
Ferguson High School, 87
Fern Ridge High School, 47, **87**, 169
Ferrand and Fitch, 118
First Public High School (Benton School), 8, 10, **77**, 163, 167
Franklin High School, 88
Froebel, Friedrich, 9
Furlong and Brown, 25, 81

Gallaudet School, 88
Garfield, President James A., 42
Gateway Academy Chesterfield, 28, 52, **132-133**
Gateway Institute Of Technology, 36, 62, 75, **88-89**, 92, 94, 167
Gateway Michael Elementary/Middle School, 67, 69, **89**
Gateway Michael High School, 67, 69, **89**
Gaunt High School (*see* W. F. Gaunt H.S.)
German-General Protestant Orphans Home (*see also* Protestant Children's Home), 68, 139

Hadley Vocational High School, 28, 35, 36, 81, **89-90**, 94, 119, 167
Hancock, General Winfield Scott, 42
Hancock High School, 90
Hancock Senior High, 25, 39, 43, **90-91**, 169
Haulter High School, 102
Hazelwood High School, 91
Hazelwood Central High, 43, **91**, 169

Hazelwood East High, 43, **91**, 169
Hazelwood West High, 43, **92**, 169
Health Careers Program High School, 92
Hellmuth and Hellmuth, 25-26, 128
"High School" (St. Louis High School – *see* Central High School, 1856)
High School Branch High Schools, 12, **32**
Hill, Gale A. and Associates, 25, 109
Hiram Neuwoehner School, 68, **92**
Hoffman/Saur & Associates, 107
HOK (Hellmuth Obata Kassabaum), 26, 106, 145
Hungate, Judge William L., 61
Huning, Charles, 26

Incarnate Word Academy, 33, 52, **133**
Ittner, William B., 13, **21-22, 26**, 31, 71, 83 110

James B. Eads High School, 32
Jefferson, President Thomas, 7
Jennings High School, 44, **93**, 169
Jennings, James, 44
"Jim Crow" laws, 59
John Burroughs School, 27, 53, **154**
John F. Kennedy Catholic High School, 133-134
John M. Vogt High School, 42, 82, 97, **93**, 169
John O'Fallon Technical High School, 93-94

Kain High School, **133-134**, 140
Kennedy Associates, Inc., 27, 119
Kennedy High School (*see* John F. Kennedy H.S.)
Kenrick-Glennon Seminary, 70, **134**, 145
Kenrick High School, 134
Kiel, Mayor Henry 66
Kinloch High School, 42, 78, **94-95**, 169
Kirkwood High School, 95
Kirkwood Military Academy, 7
Kirkwood Senior High, 44, **95**, 121, 169
Kirkwood Seminary, 7
Klutho, Victor K., 27, 127

LaBeaume and Klein, 27, 154
Laboure High School, 33, 125, 126, **135**, 147, 165
Laclède, Pierre de, **5-6**, 8
Laclède Primary School, 8
Ladue Horton Watkins High School, 45, **95-96**, 169
Lafayette High School, 96
Lafayette Senior High, 49, 86, **96**, 169
Lakeside Center of St. Louis County *(School for Boys)*, 69, **97**
La Pierre, Professor D. Bruce, 61
Leimkuehler, F. Ray, 27, 93
Liddell *vs.* Board of Education, 60
Lincoln High School/Lincoln Opportunity High School, 97
Lindbergh Senior High, 45, **97**, 169

Link and Rosenheim, 22
Litzsinger School, 68, **98**
Logos School, 53, **154**
Loretto Academy, 135
Louisiana Purchase (The), 7
Louisiana Purchase Exposition (*see also* World's Fair), 15
Lutheran Central High School, 53, **135**
Lutheran High School, 135
Lutheran North High School, 53, **136**
Lutheran South High School, 53, **136**

Mackey Mitchell Associates, 27, 128
Malone, Annie (*see* Annie Malone Children's Home)
Maplewood-Richmond Heights High School, 45, **98**, 169
Marquette Senior High, 49, **98-99**, 169
Martin Luther King, Jr., High School, 99
Mary Institute, 10, 17, 53, **154-155**, 156
Mary Institute Country Day, 53, **155-156**
Mass Media High School Program, 99
Mauran, Russell and Garden, 27, 156
McBride High School, 33, 99, 117, 118, 134, **136-137**, 165
McCluer High School, 42, 72, 87, **99**, 169
McCluer North High School, 42, 95, **100**, 169
McCluer South Berkeley, 42, 72, **100**, 169
McKinley High School, 19, 23, 63, 71, 99, **100-101**, 163, 167
McNamara, J. H., 128
Meachum, John Berry, 58
Meda P. Washington High School Program, 101
Meet Me in St. Louis, 16-18
Mehl, Charles, 45
Mehlville High School, 101
Mehlville Senior High, 46, **101-102**, 169
Melvin Ray Eskridge High School, 51, **102**, 169
Mercy Catholic High School, **137**, 140, 148, 149
Meredith, Judge James H., 60
Metro Academic and Classical High School, 63, **102-103**
Metro Academic and Classical High School Program, 102
MICDS, 17, 53, 155, 156
Michael, Elias, 66
Miller Career Academy (*see* Clyde C. Miller Career Academy)
Milligan, Rockwell M., **24**, 31, 77, 111, 119
Missouri Baptist Children's Home, 68, **137**
Missouri Compromise, 8, 12, 59
Missouri School for the Blind, 103, 155
Missouri School for the Deaf, 16
Missouri Statehood, 8
Mitchell Hudgeback, 26, 153, 158
Mount Providence Boys School, 68, **137**
Murphy and Mackey, 26

Nerinx Hall High School, 33, 52, **137-138**
Neuwoehner School (*see* Hiram Neuwoehner School)
New City School, 17, 18, 32, 155
Normal School, 9, **103**, 113
Normandy Senior High School, **104**, 169
Normandy Technical School, 46, **104**, 169
North County Christian School, 138
North County Technical, 36, **105**
North Side Catholic High School, 33, **138**
Northview High School, 28, 69, **105**
Northwest High School, 26, 54, **105-106**, 167
Notre Dame High School, 33, 52, **138**, 165

Oakville Senior High School, 45, **106**, 169
O'Fallon Technical High School (*see* John O'Fallon Technical H.S.),
Opportunity Alternative High School Program, 106

Parkway Central High School, 47, 106, **107**, 169
Parkway High School, 107
Parkway Junior-Senior High School, 106
Parkway North High School, 47, **107**, 169
Parkway South High School, 47, **108**, 169
Parkway West High School, 47, 107, **108**, 169
Parsons Brickerhoff, 25, 109
Pattonville High School, 109
Pattonville Senior High School, 23, 25, 47, **109**, 169
Peabody Branch High School, 12
Pearce and Pearce, 118
Peter and Paul High School (*see* Kenrick H.S.)
Plessy *v.* Ferguson, 59
Polytechnic Branch High School, 12, **103**
Poro College, 19, **156**
Principia (The), 19, **139**, 165
Priory, 26, 52, **145**
Protestant Children's Home, **139**, 68
Pruitt Alternative High School, 109
Public Safety and Junior NROTC High School Program, 109-110
Public School Library, 110

Ritenour High School, 110
Ritenour Senior High School, 26, 46, 48, **110**, 169
Ritter, Cardinal Joseph Elmer, 60
Ritter High School (*see* Cardinal Ritter College Prep)
Riverview Gardens Senior High School, 49, **110-111**, 169
Rock Spring Alternative High School, 111
Rockwood Summit Senior High School, 49, **111**, 169
Roosevelt High School, 24, 111-112, 113, 115, 163
Rosary High School, **140**, 148, 149
Rosati High School, 133, **140**
Rosati-Kain High School, 19, **140**, 165
Rumbold, William, 27, 80

St. Alphonsus Liguori (Rock) High School, 141
St. Anthony of Padua High School, 141
St. Charles High School, 112
St. Charles Military Academy, 7
St. Charles West High School, 112
St. Elizabeth Academy, 14, **141-142**, 165
St. Ferdinand Academy, 70
St. Francis Borgia High School, 142
St. Francis deSales High School, 33, **142**
St. John the Baptist High School, 32, **142**, 165
St. John Vianney High School, 52, **143**
St. Joseph Academy, 7, 10, 37, 52, **143**
St. Joseph Convent of Mercy, 70
St. Joseph High School, 143-144
St. Joseph Institute for the Deaf, 68, **144**
St. Joseph's Home for Boys, 144
St. Louis Academy, 7, 10, 37, 52, **144**
St. Louis Christian Home, 68, 128, **144**
St. Louis Colored Orphans Home, 113
St. Louis Country Day School (*see also*, Country Day,
    MICDS), 17, 19, 53, 155, **156**
St. Louis Preparatory Seminary North, 144-145
St. Louis Preparatory Seminary South, 145
St. Louis Priory (*see* Priory)
St. Louis University High School, 7, 10, **146**, 165
St. Louis Vocational Special School, 68
St. Mark the Evangelist High School, 146
St. Mary's High School, 33, **146**, 164
St. Mary's Orphan Home, 147
St. Mary's Special School for Exceptional Children, 147
St. Peter High School (*see* Coyle H.S.)
St. Philomena Technical School, 36, 85, **147**
St. Stanislaus Seminary, 70, **147-148**
St. Theresa Academy, 148
St. Thomas Aquinas High School, 52, 137, **148**
St. Thomas Aquinas-Mercy High School, 52, 137, 140,
    148, 149
St. Vincent Home for Children, 149
St. Xavier High School, 149
Sanger, George W., 28, 89, 115
Schoolhouse No. 1, 8
Schoolhouse No. 3, 8, 77
Senior Classical Academic High School Program 113
Simon, Shulamith, 61
Smith Academy and Manual Training School, 18, 19, 78,
    127, **156**
Smith, Elizabeth, 48
Soldan-Blewett High School, 32, 78, 79, 113-114
Soldan High School, 18, 19, 23, 31, 71, 75, 78, 79, 80, 113
Soldan International High School Studies Program, 114
South County Technical, 28, 36, **114**
Southern High School, 83, 84
South Grand Work-Study High School Program, 115
Southview School, 68, **115**
Southwest High School, 28, 31, 33, 80, 82, 84, 85, **115**,

116, 167
Special School District, 36, 67, 69
Stander and Sons, 28, 130
Stix, Rachel, 66
Sumner High School, 13, 14, 19, 23, 59, 71, 86, 88, 94,
    116-117

Taylor, Isaac, 24, 25
The Churchill School, 157
The Priory (*see* Priory)
Thomas Jefferson School, 157
Tower Grove Christian School, 149
Tri-A Outreach Center I High School Program, 117
Tri-A Outreach Center II High School Program, 117-118
Trinity Catholic High School, 52, 72, 140, 148, **149**
Truteau, Jean Baptiste, 6
Turner Open Air School, 118
Tyrer, Jack, 28, 132

University City Senior High School, 49, **118**, 169
Upper Louisiana Territory, 7
Ursuline Academy, 7, 10, 37, 52, 130, **150**

Valley Park Senior High, 118-119
Vashon High School, 24, 60, 72, 81, 84, 90, **119-120**,
    157, 167
Vianney High School (*see* St. John Vianney HS)
Villa Duchesne, 33, 53, 123, 124, 129, **150**
Virtual high schools, 75
Visitation Academy, 10, 17, 24, 37, 53, **151**, 165
Vogt High School (*see* John M. Vogt H.S.)

Wade Branch High School, 32
Washington High School, 120
Washington Vocational High School (*see* B. T.
    Washington Vocational H.S.)
Webster Branch High School, 12
Webster Groves High School, 50, 86, **120-121**, 169
Wells, Erastus, 50
Wellston High School, 51, **121**, 169
West County Technical, 36, **121-122**, 152
Westminster Christian Academy, 122, **151-152**
W. F. Gaunt High School (*see also* Affton High School),
    40, 169
Whitfield School, 158
Wischmeyer, Kenneth, 28, 105, 114,136
World's Fair, 15-19
World War II, 37
Wyman Hall School, 10, 26, 53, **158**

Xavier High School (*see* St. Xavier)

Yeatman High School, 17, 19, 23, 81, 82, 101, **122**,
    163, 167
Yeshiva (*see* Block Yeshiva High School)

Other titles available from Virginia Publishing Company

Twenty Years of J.C.: The Man, The Legend, The Lawsuit

Lost Caves of St. Louis

Meeting Louis at the Fair

Meet Me in St. Louis

Still Shining! Lost Treasures of the 1904 World's Fair

Queen of Lace: The Story of the Continental Life Building

The Streets of St. Louis

Made in USA: The Story of East St. Louis

Greg Freeman: A Gentleman, A Gentle Man

Spirits of St. Louis

Spirits of St. Louis II

Beyond Gooey Butter Cake

Tales from the Coral Court

and many more local stories by local authors!

www.STL-BOOKS.com